Cu
Mu

Robin Ireland

Cutting the Mustard

50 Years of Dreaming

From fans to consumers: The story of the commercialisation of English football through five rollercoaster decades of Norwich City – from Division One to the Premier League, the UEFA Cup and beyond

Robin Ireland

AXIS PROJECTS PUBLISHING

First published in the
United Kingdom by
Axis Projects Publishing
c/o www.alanjward.co.uk

ISBN: 978-1-9164089-3-7 paperback

British Library Cataloguing-in-Publication
Data. A catalogue record for this book is
available from the British Library

Design & Layout: AJW assisted by
SFW @ alanjward.co.uk

Typefaces: text - Nudica sans,
headlines - Arsenica Variable

Materials
Text: Arctic Volume 150gsm,
Cover: silk art 300gsm,
(both FSC MIX)

Print: Gomer Press, Wales

All author and press enquiries:
robin@robinireland.com

COYY

Player cards:
(Topps Chewing Gum)
Author's collection

Contents

Introduction

In 1972 Norwich City Football Club reached the top level of the English Football League for the first time in their history. Seventy years after their formation in 1902, the Canaries had hit the jackpot. Yet fifty years later, competing in the Premier League still seems out of reach.

Whilst Norwich could dream of finishing high enough to qualify for Europe in the 1980s and 1990s, huge injections of money into football, based on broadcasting contracts and commercial revenues, have made competition at the top level of English football a distant memory for all but a handful of clubs. So, how did this happen?

This book looks back at five decades of dreaming in yellow and green from the heady excitement of that first season in Division One to the pandemic years of 2020 and 2021, when football, like every other aspect of society, came under the microscope. To slightly misquote Bill Shankly: for a time, football really was about life and death.

But this is really the story of the commercialisation and the selling of English football: how football supporters have been transformed from fans into consumers, and how every aspect of the football business has been costed to maximise profits – from replica shirts to ticket prices. The majority of the owners of clubs in the top two leagues are now based overseas, and the biggest television audiences are not even in Europe. Today's kick-off times reflect programming schedules, not the interests of fans. And it is all about money.

The 1970s and 1980s were dark days for football in England. The excitement of the World Cup victory in 1966 seemed a long way back, firmly in the rear-view mirror. Crowds were declining, stadiums decaying, and racism and violence were ever present in the murky, dark cloud that surrounded football. Margaret Thatcher's government did not like the sport or its fans, and it took a series of terrible disasters for change to happen, and for English football's rebirth.

For one brief decade in the 1990s football and Britain became cool again. Norwich City led the newly formed Premier League for the majority of the 1992/93 season. They could even dream briefly of European glory. But the excitement didn't last for long – the club was facing bankruptcy in 1996, when Delia Smith and her husband, Michael Wynn-Jones, first joined the Norwich City board.

Tony Blair's Labour Party landslide General Election win in 1997 changed nothing for football: he continued the Conservative Party's policies of selling off many of our national assets, whilst allowing global markets to determine the direction of the economy. And, as we entered the twenty-first century, the financial meltdown of the banks impacted on all aspects of society. Foreign billionaires – even states – started to buy into the English game, transforming it for ever.

Now, post-COVID, with Delia and Michael standing down after twenty-eight years of majority ownership at Norwich City, it's time for the club to look ahead and determine the future direction. But that is so much harder than it might have appeared in 1972. The stakes are higher, the risks greater, and the footballing landscape has been transformed.

Whilst *Cutting the Mustard* tells the Norwich City story, it could be the story of most other English provincial clubs: Burnley, Watford, West Bromwich Albion and Sheffield United have yo-yoed between the Championship and the Premier League in recent years. Others such as Huddersfield Town, Derby County, Wigan and Portsmouth have invested considerable sums to reach the top, only to fall back, exhausted from their efforts.

The days of Wolverhampton Wanderers or even Leicester City winning the league are long gone. We are faced with a future in which a European Super League exists, even if it is not explicitly called that, when younger fans are often priced out of attending, and when television audiences are prioritised above all else.

So perhaps it is time to examine more closely how this happened. And how it came to pass that the dreams of so many were sold to serve the interests of the very few. This book explores the changes in English football and encourages all those who care about the sport to speak out about how it should be governed in the future.

Admiral

THE 1970s

Selling the Unsellable

Selling the Unsellable

1970 The FIFA World Cup in Mexico is the first to be televised in colour

1971 Ibrox disaster: 66 die in a crush at the Rangers vs Celtic match, Glasgow

1973/74 Industrial action under Edward Heath's government leads to a three-day week

1974 João Havelange is elected president of FIFA, replacing Sir Stanley Rous and serving until 1998; Birmingham pub bombings carried out by the Provisional IRA

1975 The Football Trust is set up by the government with funding from pools companies to assist with the costs of implementing the Safety of Sports Grounds Act 1975

1977 The Anti-Nazi League is formed to oppose the rise of far-right racist groups

1978 Following a ruling by the European Community in February, the Football League lifts its ban on foreign players; Viv Anderson becomes the first black player to win a senior England cap

1978/79 'Winter of Discontent' under James Callaghan's government

1979 Trevor Francis becomes Britain's first million-pound footballer when he is transferred from Birmingham City to Nottingham Forest; Margaret Thatcher is elected UK Prime Minister in May 1979; Liverpool announce a one-year £50,000 deal with Japanese electrical giant Hitachi to wear the company's name on their shirts

Previous spread: Norwich City's first Admiral strip worn between 1976 and 1981 (replica). Leeds United had signed the first deal with Admiral in 1974. Background: the cover of the match programme for Norwich City vs Manchester United, 2 April 1977

Author's collections

The highs and lows of the 1970s

The 1970s were challenging times in the United Kingdom. Everything seemed to be in black and white, with successive governments enmeshed with challenging industrial relations, bombings on mainland Britain reflecting the Troubles in Northern Ireland, and rubbish piled high on the streets by the end of the decade.

Following England's success on home soil in 1966, the country's national sport seemed to go downhill pretty swiftly afterwards. The 1970 World Cup in Mexico might have been broadcast in glorious technicolour for the first time, but very few people had colour television sets to view England's 2–3 capitulation to West Germany, with Peter Bonetti having replaced Gordon Banks in goal.

Despite the downfall of the national team on our screens, English club football was full of larger-than-life figures, who realised that there were opportunities to make money both on and off the pitch. The potential of the new television football consumer was clearly going to change the game hugely, and there were a range of entrepreneurs eyeing up the prospects eagerly. At international level, England's Sir Stanley Rous, who represented the old school of the game perfectly, was replaced as UEFA president by Brazilian João Havelange, who based his pitch to FIFA's member associations on exploiting the commercial opportunities of the global game.

Meanwhile club football was played on pitches that cut up into mud-baths in the winter, in front of spectators who often came as much for a fight as a game of football. Racism accompanied the violence inside and outside the grounds, even as clubs were desperate to bring income into the game as match attendances slumped. The election of Margaret Thatcher in 1979 indicated the future direction of travel of both society and football.

Pre-1972 pin badges

Author's collection

Against this volatile backdrop of rapid decline across the United Kingdom, it was nevertheless an exciting decade for Norwich City as they won promotion to Division One for the first time.

First Division First-Timers

Norwich City were promoted to the First Division under manager Ron Saunders, after finishing as Second Division champions in April 1972. Saunders had been appointed in July 1969 by chairman Geoffrey Watling, and in season 1972/73 they reached the top level of English

First home game programme in the top flight, featuring the new club badge. Norwich City vs Everton Saturday 12th August 1972

Author's collection

A Norwich City rosette worn in the 1960s/70s featuring the design worn on the players' shirts. A new badge for the club was worn from the 1972/73 season

Author's collection

The design featured a canary perched on a ball under Norwich Castle with a lion passant, and was the work of architect Andrew Anderson. Anderson received a payment of £10 for the use of the design[1]

1 James Woodrow (as compiled for the Norwich City Football Club), *Norwich City Football Club: The Archive* (Severn, 2022), vol. II, 11 March 1972.

NORWICH CITY
FOOTBALL CLUB
First Division v EVERTON
Carrow Road, Saturday, 12th Aug. 1972
kick-off 3 pm
7p
Official Match-day Programme
Volume 1 Number 1

football for the first time. Their preparations included building a police control centre and a permanent platform for television cameras in the South Stand, at a cost of about £7,000.[2]

Only a year later, in March 1973, City made their first appearance at Wembley, losing 0–1 to Tottenham Hotspur in the Football League Cup Final. Watling stood down as chairman in the summer of the same year, with former Lord Mayor and Labour leader of Norwich City Council Arthur South taking his position. Manager and chairman swiftly fell out, and Saunders left the club in November 1973 following a 1–3 home defeat to Everton. Although new manager John Bond could not prevent relegation at the end of the season, Norwich were swiftly promoted again in April 1975, having finished third in Division Two behind Manchester United and Aston Villa. Bond was a character made for 1970s football – all sideburns, coiffed hair, cigars and expensive suits. Like even bigger names such as Malcolm Allison and Tommy Docherty, Bond was willing to embrace the wider opportunities that the increasing media coverage of football offered.

World Cup Willies

England's World Cup triumph in 1966 both helped glamorise football and acts as a marker in the growing commercialisation of the game. UEFA had been formed in 1954, and the establishment of its club competitions in 1955 was critical in the developing power and economic base of pan-European football. At the same time, the introduction of television and the growth of broadcasting into homes transformed the experience of watching football. As the sociologist David Goldblatt writes, the 1960 European Cup Final between Real Madrid and Eintracht Frankfurt was the first to be broadcast live across the Continent.[3] Fifteen million people in the UK watched England win the World Cup in 1966, although in black and white. The first World Cup Final to be broadcast in colour took place four years later in 1970 in Mexico, when Brazil beat Italy 4–1. Brazil's famous yellow shirts were seen in their full glory, and their final goal lived long in the memory, with Pelé laying off a sublime pass to Carlos Alberto who did not need to break stride before cracking the ball low and hard into the net.

World Cup Willie – the official mascot of the 1966 World Cup held in England (despite the Union Jack on Willie's shirt)

Author's collection

2 Ibid., vol. II, 10 August 1972.

3 David Goldblatt, *The Ball is Round: A Global History of Football* (Penguin, 2007).

Some academics such as Roger Domeneghetti argue that it was the 1966 World Cup in England which established the template for televised football.[4] Whilst there were 91,000 inside Wembley Stadium, another 400 million people around the world were watching. This global audience for football led to the explosion in the commercialisation of the game. The 1966 World Cup introduced several innovations, including changes of kick-off times to suit television and give better viewing figures, a live draw for the tournament, and seedings to keep the favourites apart. It also featured the first televised action replays, which immediately increased the entertainment value for watchers. The English Football Association produced the first World Cup mascot for the tournament. World Cup Willie, a cartoon lion with a Union Jack (not the flag of St George) on its chest, appeared on all kinds of merchandise from badges and soft toys to beer mats and tea trays. FIFA ensured that it had asserted its rights over the global commercial exploitation of the tournament for the 1970 World Cup. FIFA was to lead the way in the exploitation of football in the future, after the Englishman, Sir Stanley Rous, lost the election for president in 1974 to João Havelange. Rous lost because of both his perceived conservatism and his identification with apartheid and the racial segregation of the game in South Africa.[5] But Havelange also built his bid for the FIFA presidency on the commercial development of football based on the sale of broadcasting rights and the accompanying sponsorship income.[6] In contrast, in 1966, the BBC was still able to insist there was no pitchside advertising at the World Cup in England.

Player card (Topps Chewing Gum)

Author's collection

Cup Runs

Norwich City built a reputation for cup success following on from their remarkable progress in the 1958/59 FA Cup, when they reached the semi-final whilst still a Division Three team, beating Manchester United and Tottenham Hotspur on the way. The club also won the second staging of the Football League Cup, which had been established in 1960/61 in response to the popularity of European football, and as part of a suggested new football structure to revamp the leagues in English football.[7] The idea for the new League Cup competition had been put

4 Roger Domeneghetti, *From the Back Page to the Front Room: Football's Journey through the English Media* (Ockley Books, 2014).

5 Paul Darby, 'Stanley Rous's "own goal": football politics, South Africa and the contest for the FIFA presidency in 1974', in Dolores Martinez and Projit B. Mukharji (eds), *Football: From England to the World* (Routledge, 2013).

6 John Sugden and Alan Tomlinson, *FIFA and the Contest for World Football: Who Rules the People's Game?* (Polity, 1998).

forward by Stanley Rous and then enacted by the Football League's secretary, Alan Hardaker. Norwich, then in the Second Division, won a two-leg final against Fourth Division Rochdale in the second season of the staging of the Football League Cup in 1962; Aston Villa had won the inaugural trophy.

Whilst neither the FA Cup nor the League Cup were sponsored at this time, there were no similar hindrances to the Texaco Cup, which was one of the first English football competitions to receive commercial sponsorship (the Watney Cup was the first in 1970). The American petroleum company Texaco sponsored the competition to the tune of £100,000, and this was intended to help promote Texaco's purchase of Regent filling stations, according to Jim Heath of *When Saturday Comes*. As Heath writes, the Texaco Cup might be argued to be the beginning of the modernisation of the game.[8] The late Denis Howell (the then Sports Minister), who was to lead an inquiry into sports sponsorship in 1983, is quoted as saying: 'The one event that I do not expect to see sponsored in my lifetime is the FA Cup itself, it would hardly be British, though I would not be surprised to find the sponsorship of individual clubs as a future development.'[9] In fact, it was only eleven years later that the FA Cup received its first sponsorship from Littlewoods Pools. It was known as the FA Cup sponsored by Littlewoods from the 1994/95 season to 1997/98.

Match day ticket from one of Norwich City's cup games in the '70s

Author's collection

The Texaco Cup initially involved the top teams from England, Scotland, Northern Ireland and the Republic of Ireland who had not qualified for European competition. Nowadays UEFA's Europa Conference League (its third-tier competition) provides a similar opportunity for less successful clubs across Europe (although West Ham United were delighted to win the trophy in 2023). The Irish clubs had withdrawn by 1972/73 because of the Troubles, making it an Anglo-Scottish affair (indeed, once Texaco's sponsorship ended it became the Anglo-Scottish Cup). Football club programmes were developing at this time and beginning to offer more opportunities to advertisers and sponsors. Texaco provided a common style of outer covers for the programmes for its competition. Each club taking part received £1,000, with higher payments resulting from tournament success.[10]

7 Rob Carless, *Under the Floodlights! The Story of the English Football League Cup 1960–2024* (Pitch Publishing, 2024).

8 Jim Heath, 'Best of British oils', *When Saturday Comes*, 173 (July 2001). Available at: https://www.wsc.co.uk/the-archive/best-of-british-oils/ (accessed 14 May 2025).

9 Quoted in ibid.

10 Woodrow, *Norwich City Football Club*, vol. II, 13 September 1972.

The outer cover (front and back) of the match programme for The Texaco Cup Second Round Second Leg, Norwich City vs Leicester City, Wednesday 8th November 1972

Author's collection

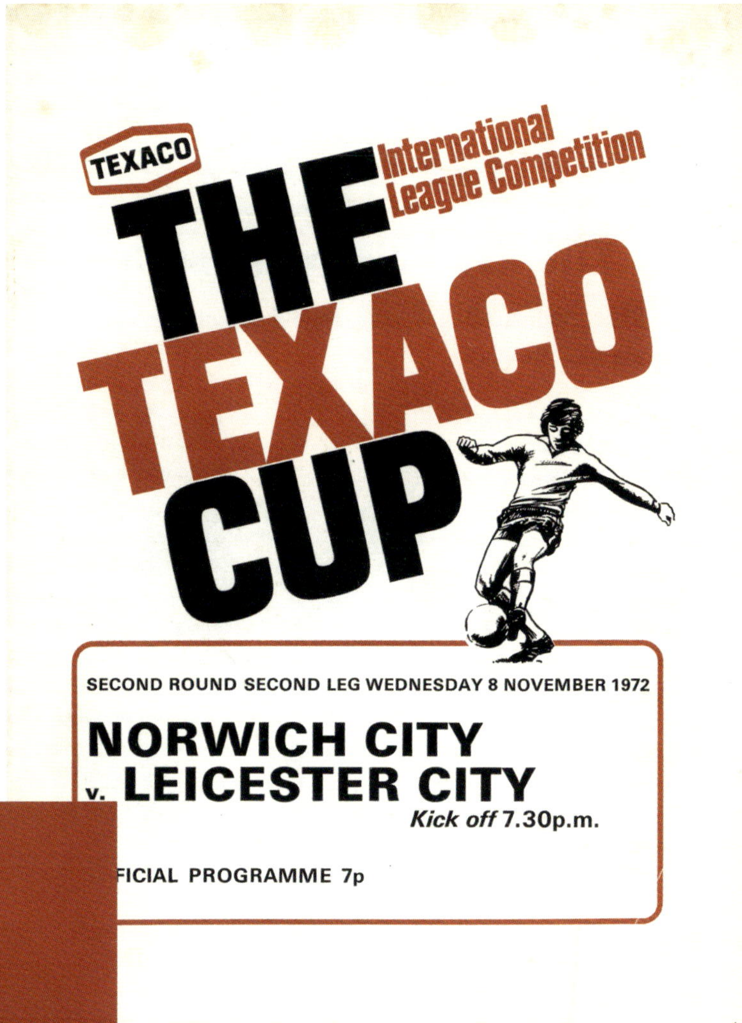

Norwich had considerable success in cup competitions in the 1970s, appearing in the two-legged Texaco Cup Final in 1973, and in two League Cup Finals in 1973 and 1975. Sadly, they lost all four matches. The cup runs contributed significantly to gate receipts in City's annual accounts published in 1973: £137,825 in total. Television and broadcasting fees were recorded at about £7,200.[11]

Match Report: Saturday 3 March 1973, k/o 15:30.
The Football League Cup Final, Wembley Empire Stadium,
Norwich City 0 Tottenham Hotspur 1. Attendance: 100,000.

Norwich City
Kevin Keelan, Clive Payne, Geoff Butler, Dave Stringer, Duncan Forbes, Max Briggs, Doug Livermore, Jim Blair (Trevor Howard), David Cross, Graham Paddon, Terry Anderson. Manager: Ron Saunders.

Tottenham Hotspur
Pat Jennings, Joe Kinnear, Cyril Knowles, John Pratt (Ralph Coates), Mike England, Phil Beal, Alan Gilzean, Steve Perryman, Martin Chivers, Martin Peters, Jimmy Pearce. Manager: Bill Nicholson.

Goals
Tottenham Hotspur: Coates (72)

Norwich City's first ever season as a Division One team following their promotion under Ron Saunders in 1971/72 was certainly full of highs and lows. They drew their first game in the top division 1–1 against Everton, and followed up with a 2–1 win at Ipswich with goals from Jimmy Bone and Terry Anderson. Home wins over Tottenham and Arsenal in the autumn showed that the newly promoted side were not overawed by their surroundings. Arguably, the Canaries' successes in the early rounds of both the League Cup and the Texaco Cup and the additional matches that resulted might have affected their league performances, and between mid-November and mid-April Norwich had no league victories and were at serious risk of relegation. Norwich faced Leeds United (this was Leeds United in their pomp under Don Revie) three times in January in the third round of the FA Cup, eventually losing a calamitous second replay 0–5.

Norwich's opening match in that season's League Cup was in the second round when they beat Leicester City 2–1 (with a brace by Jimmy

11 Ibid., vol. II, 1 August 1973.

Player cards (Topps Chewing Gum)

At the heart of the Norwich City defence in their promotion-winning season of 1971-72. All three (inc. David Stringer overleaf) also played in City's two Wembley appearances in the 1970s and Kevin Keelan went on to make a record 673 appearances for the club.

Author's collection

Bone) on 6 September at Carrow Road. By March 1973 Norwich had also overcome Hull City, Stockport County, Arsenal and Chelsea on their path to the final. The semi-final against Chelsea was played over two legs, with the second match at Carrow Road abandoned because of fog with Norwich leading. There were no problems in the replayed second leg – rather surprisingly watched by Prince Andrew[12] – with the Norfolk side securing their first ever appearance at Wembley. This was then still called the Wembley Empire Stadium (the stadium was celebrating its 50th anniversary, having been built in 1923).

Norwich City were certainly the underdogs in the final. Tottenham had not deigned to enter during the first six years of the Football League Cup, but had then won the competition in 1971, and were semi-finalists in 1969 and 1972. Spurs' legendary manager, Bill Nicholson, already had a tremendous cup history including winning the inaugural UEFA Cup in 1972 (it had previously been known as the European Fairs Cup). At the very least, both teams had the opportunity to win the trophy for the second time, Norwich having also been victorious in 1962.

The 1973 League Cup Final was televised live in colour, with an estimated 45,000 Canaries fans making the trip to Wembley. The match programme noted that the City side that beat Chelsea cost a total of £169,000, a fraction of what Tottenham had spent on team-building in the previous decade. Norwich's biggest signing to play on the day was David Cross, who had cost £40,000 when he arrived from Rochdale in October 1971. Norwich were captained by Duncan Forbes, with the team including Kevin Keelan, Geoff Butler, Dave Stringer and Graham Paddon. Meanwhile the Tottenham side contained eight full internationals, and they were captained by World Cup winner Martin Peters. Ralph Coates, better recalled perhaps these days for his impressive combover hairstyle, was a record signing for Tottenham from Burnley for a fee of £190,000 in May 1971. Colin Suggett had been signed by the Canaries from West Bromwich Albion for £70,000 in February 1973 but was ineligible to play (as was Trevor Hockey), as he had played for his previous club in an earlier round.

The match unfortunately was not long remembered, as it was generally considered a little disappointing, with neither side at their best. Whilst Graham Paddon had scored two brilliant free kicks that had been captured earlier in the season by Anglia TV's Match of the Week,[13] there was sadly no recurrence of his heroics for the Norwich

12 Ibid., vol. II, 3 January 1973.

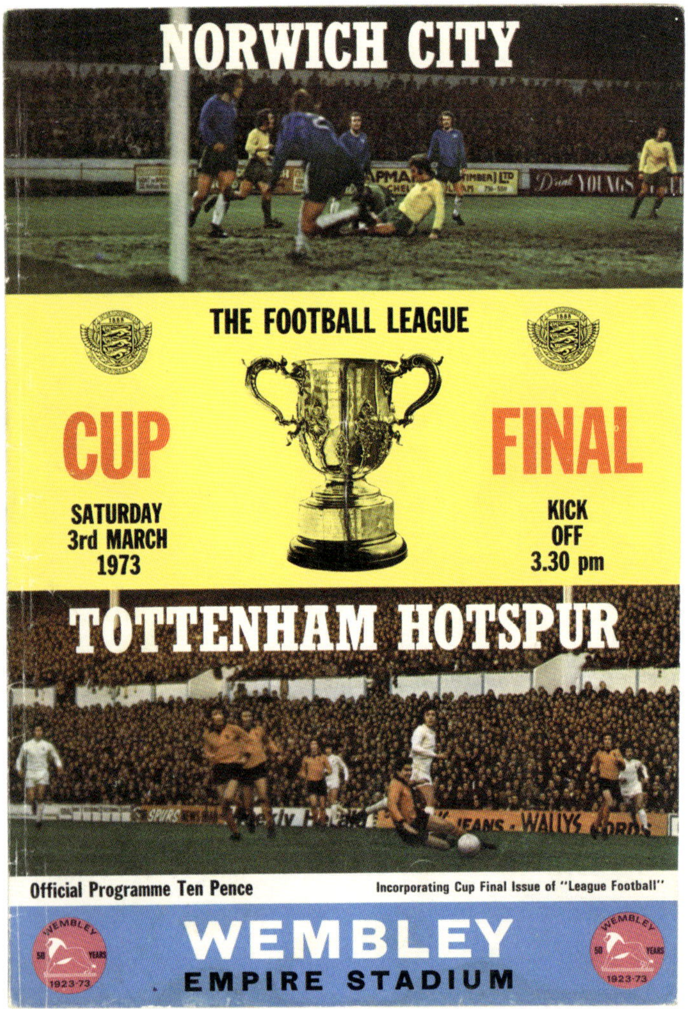

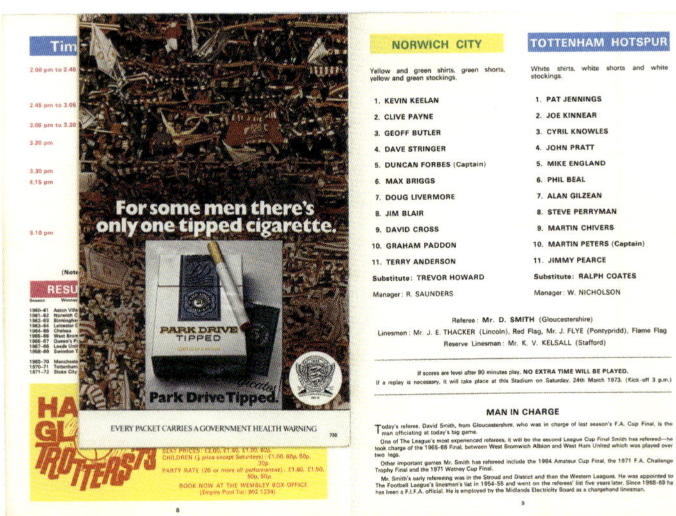

NORWICH CITY

Yellow and green shirts, green shorts, yellow and green stockings.

1. KEVIN KEELAN
2. CLIVE PAYNE
3. GEOFF BUTLER
4. DAVE STRINGER
5. DUNCAN FORBES (Captain)
6. MAX BRIGGS
7. DOUG LIVERMORE
8. JIM BLAIR
9. DAVID CROSS
10. GRAHAM PADDON
11. TERRY ANDERSON

Substitute: TREVOR HOWARD

Manager: R. SAUNDERS

TOTTENHAM HOTSPUR

White shirts, white shorts and white stockings.

1. PAT JENNINGS
2. JOE KINNEAR
3. CYRIL KNOWLES
4. JOHN PRATT
5. MIKE ENGLAND
6. PHIL BEAL
7. ALAN GILZEAN
8. STEVE PERRYMAN
9. MARTIN CHIVERS
10. MARTIN PETERS (Captain)
11. JIMMY PEARCE

Substitute: RALPH COATES

Manager: W. NICHOLSON

Referee: **Mr. D. SMITH** (Gloucestershire)

Linesmen: Mr. J. E. THACKER (Lincoln), Red Flag, Mr. J. FLYE (Pontypridd), Flame Flag

Reserve Linesman: Mr. K. V. KELSALL (Stafford)

If scores are level after 90 minutes play, **NO EXTRA TIME WILL BE PLAYED.**
If a replay is necessary, it will take place at this Stadium on Saturday, 24th March 1973. (Kick-off 3 p.m.)

MAN IN CHARGE

Today's referee, David Smith, from Gloucestershire, who was in charge of last season's F.A. Cup Final, is the man officiating at today's big game.

One of The League's most experienced referees, it will be the second League Cup Final Smith has refereed—he took charge of the 1965-66 Final, between West Bromwich Albion and West Ham United which was played over two legs.

Other important games Mr. Smith has refereed include the 1964 Amateur Cup Final, the 1971 F.A. Challenge Trophy Final and the 1971 Watney Cup Final.

Mr. Smith's early refereeing was in the Stroud and District and then the Western Leagues. He was appointed to The Football League's linesmen's list in 1954-55 and went on the referees' list five years later. Since 1968-69 he has been a F.I.F.A. official. He is employed by the Midlands Electricity Board as a chargehand linesman.

9

Top: The cover of the 1972/73 Football League Cup Final match programme. Below: Rear cover of League Football – insert into the Cup Final programme

Author's collection

Player card
(Topps Chewing Gum)
Author's collection

fans to celebrate at Wembley. In the 73rd minute a long throw from Martin Chivers was nudged on by Martin Peters. The ball was cleared but was met by Ralph Coates, a first-half substitute, whose right-footed shot from the edge of the penalty area evaded an attempted block by Terry Anderson and a diving Kevin Keelan to find the bottom corner. A poor match was enlivened by Brian Moore's commentary: 'A beautiful shot by Coates, the substitute scores a cracking goal.'[14] *The comments from the Norwich players after the match suggested that it was 'not a classic' (Dave Stringer) and that 'I think we left it on the training ground' (David Cross).*[15] *Chivers (later to play for Norwich) summed up the goal succinctly: 'Late in the game I took a long throw. The ball was partially cleared to the edge of the area and Ralph belted it into the net. His hair went mad as he went on his famous run.'*

The match programme and the accompanying League Football magazine insert are chock full of advertisements from companies wishing to address the young male market for 1970s football. There are advertisements for Littlewoods Pools, Castella cigars ('makes a good time great'), Double Diamond pale ale, Bells whisky, and two brands of cigarettes (Players No.6 and Park Drive). The League Football insert also carries an inside front cover colour advert for the Texaco Cup ('Something for footballers to drive for') and a two-page ad for the Watney Cup (named after the Watney Mann brewery and the first English football competition to sell its naming rights). The advertisement copy read, 'The Watney Cup is the first sponsored UK football event to guarantee goals.' This is because it was the first competition to introduce a penalty shootout in English football.

Violence

The fighting and 'hooliganism' of this era have been much considered by sociologists. Rogan Taylor, a founder member of the Football Supporters Association (FSA), which was launched in Liverpool after the Heysel Stadium disaster in 1985 and who gained his doctorate at the University of Lancaster in the same year, is one amongst many who has written about 'football hooliganism'.[16] As he points out, there had been crowd disturbances since the beginnings of the professional game, and he references train-wrecking by Liverpool and Everton fans in the 1955/56

13 Matt Eastley, *Brian Moore Saved Our Sundays: The Golden Age of Televised Football* (Pitch Publishing, 2024).

14 Quoted in ibid., p. 83.

15 The following quotations are taken from Carless, *Under the Floodlights!*, pp. 76–7.

16 Rogan Taylor, *Football and its Fans: Supporters and their Relations with the Game, 1885–1985* (Leicester University Press, 1992).

season as an example. In the 1970s Manchester United fans had built a reputation for making trouble at away games. They certainly displayed this 'talent' when playing at Carrow Road in 1977.

Taylor described a report from David Smith, the chairman of the Manchester United Supporters Club, who wrote at this time that the media bore a responsibility for some of the actions of misbehaving fans through 'biased and irresponsible publicity'.[17] The police were criticised in the same report for their aggressive tactics in seeking to address perceived trouble in the stands. Meantime, Monica Hartland of the National Federation of Football Supporters' Clubs (the forerunner of the FSA) called for a return of the birch as well as declaring that 'the main reason for hooliganism is sociologists'.[18] Presumably because they wrote about it!

The terrible state of football stadiums, the attitudes of the footballing authorities and the police towards football fans, and of course the violence of a minority of those who followed football led to the tragedies of the 1980s. They also set the scene for the transformation and, arguably, the 'bourgeoisification' of English football in the 1990s. The very term 'hooliganism' is of course loaded, and how it is used often demonstrates the political persuasion of the writer and speaker. The most common explanation of the word is that it is derived from Patrick Hoolihan (or Hooligan), an Irish hoodlam living in London in the nineteenth century. Certainly, it began to be used in the 1970s to describe crowd violence and was associated with young men from low socio-economic backgrounds. At one time hooliganism was called the 'English disease', although this pattern of behaviour was subsequently replicated across Europe.

Sociologist Richard Giulianotti is one who has explored the various explanations for football-related violence. He noted that in the 1970s, fan disorder involving Manchester United, Chelsea, Derby County, Glasgow Rangers and Millwall fans led to increasing discussions about social control interventions. A Marxist perspective on hooliganism at that time might argue that it was a young working-class backlash against 'the cultivation of a middle-class image for the game'.[19] Meantime, the tabloid press took a sensationalist populist position on misbehaving fans, in which the language they used suggested that bringing back the birch to deal with miscreants was a perfectly serious option, whilst at the same time they amplified fan violence through their high-profile coverage.

17 Quoted in ibid., p. 168.

18 Quoted in ibid., p. 169.

19 Richard Giulianotti, 'Social identity and public order', in Richard Giulianotti, Norman Bonney and Mike Hepworth (eds), *Football, Violence and Social Identity* (Routledge, 1994), p. 15.

Match Report: Saturday 2 April 1977, k/o 15:00.
League Division One, Carrow Road, Norwich City 2 Manchester United 1.
Attendance: 24,161.

Norwich City
Kevin Keelan, John Ryan, Colin Sullivan, Mel Machin, David Jones, Tony Powell, Jimmy Neighbour, Kevin Reeves, Roger Gibbins, Colin Suggett (Billy Steele), Martin Peters. Manager: John Bond.

Manchester United
Alex Stepney, Jimmy Nicholl, Stewart Houston, Sammy McIlroy, Brian Greenhoff, Martin Buchan, Steve Coppell, Jimmy Greenhoff, David McCreary, Lou Macari, Gordon Hill (Chris McGrath).
Manager: Tommy Docherty.

Goals
Norwich City: Suggett (7), Reeves (33)
Manchester United: Powell (o.g., 57)

Going to football matches in the 1970s was seriously scary, unless you were actively looking for a fight that is. As a student at nearby Norwich City College, I remember walking to the ground sometimes covering my scarf to try to avoid trouble. I vividly recall entering Norwich railway station after a match with Aston Villa when one young Norwich fan was sprinting for his life, with blood pouring down his front, with a pack of Villa supporters running after him. I was also in the Barclay Stand when there was a rumour that an away fan was using a Stanley knife to slash at our faces. In December 1975 there was fighting on the pitch between rival supporters at Carrow Road after Norwich had beaten West Ham United 1–0: 34 people were injured and 31 arrested (30 being West Ham supporters).[20] *This trouble later resulted in barriers and chain link fencing being constructed in the Barclay Stand, and ground modifications such as this, intended to separate fans and reduce the risk of crowd disorder, were a regular feature throughout the 1970s.*

But the tension and excitement caused when Manchester United were in town was at another level. The reports from Norwich City vs Manchester United in April 1977 talk of up to 15,000 Reds fans invading Carrow Road (it was probably more like 7,000). The BBC televised the match as part of a documentary it was making, and its focus was certainly not on the football being played on the pitch.

Player card (Figurine Panini, Football 78)
Author's collection

20 Woodrow, *Norwich City Football Club*, vol. II, 6 December 1975.

DONATION 40p

MARTIN

MARTIN PETERS TESTIMONIAL
SOUVENIR MATCH MAGAZINE

NORWICH CITY versus
THE 1966 ENGLAND
WORLD CUP
SQUAD

At Carrow Road
Wednesday
18th October 1978

BLUE BOAR GARAGE
(Sprowston) Ltd., Wroxham Road
Norwich. Telephone 47812

Martin Peters Testimonial Souvenir Match Magazine. Norwich City vs The 1966 England World Cup Squad, Carrow Rd., 18th October 1978

Author's collection

Tommy Docherty is well remembered for his time as manager of Manchester United. His sides were entertaining and attacking, and the Doc himself was memorably described as 'seventies man incarnate', with his kipper ties and stories of alcohol-fuelled excess.[21] *But the 1977 team weren't a patch on the United of the Best-inspired pomp of the Busby years in the 1960s. Docherty had been appointed in December 1972 and oversaw the club's relegation in 1974, although they roared back into Division One and reached the FA Cup Final in 1976, and did the same in 1977, beating Liverpool 2–1. This proved to be Docherty's final season. Nevertheless, it was still a strong team which turned out at Carrow Road, featuring the likes of Alex Stepney, Sammy McIlroy, Chris McGrath, the Greenhoff brothers and Lou Macari. They were fifth in Division One, seven points behind the leaders, Ipswich Town, but with three matches in hand. When they visited Carrow Road, United were on a 15-match unbeaten run which had also taken them into the FA Cup semi-finals. Norwich were eight points behind them in 13th place. The Norwich team featured fan favourites Kevin Keelan, Mel Machin, Jimmy Neighbour and Martin Peters.*

Norwich were lucky enough to have Peters playing for them between 1975 and 1980; he joined when the club were third in the Second Division and pushing for promotion. Peters did not fancy playing Second Division football, but he liked the set-up at the club and John Bond's playing style, so he gambled on promotion. As Peters later wrote, Bond had assured him that 'With you in the team, promotion is practically guaranteed.'[22] *And the Canaries' manager was dead right. The World Cup winner's contribution was immediate. With ten matches left in the season when he arrived in March 1975, Norwich went on to lose only two more, with Peters himself contributing two goals (in 1–0 victories over Nottingham Forest and Portsmouth). Norwich gained promotion after finishing third behind Manchester United and Aston Villa.*

Against Manchester United in April 1977 there were first-half goals for Norwich from Colin Suggett (in just the seventh minute) and the young Kevin Reeves (signed from AFC Bournemouth in February 1977 for a reported £50,000), whose goal after 33 minutes involved him rounding Martin Buchan before slotting past Alex Stepney. Despite an own goal by Tony Powell in the 57th minute, when the defender, under

21 Richard Kurt and Chris Nickeas, *The Red Army Years: Manchester United in the 1970s* (Headline, 1997), p. 4.

22 Martin Peters, *The Ghost of '66: The Autobiography* (Orion Books, 2006), p. 246.

pressure from Stewart Houston, looped a header over Kevin Keelan, City held on to claim the two points.

But the match is not remembered for the score but for what happened after it had finished. The mufcinfo website sums this up succinctly: 'Utd. fans tear at the Barclay stand throwing missiles & using planks as weapons. An 18-year-old Utd fan from Bradford climbs on the stand before falling 40 feet onto the concrete below. He was helped by St John Ambulance before he was attacked by the home fans.'[23] There is a YouTube clip of the game entitled 'Hooligans'. It is two minutes forty-five seconds long but features no football action at all. The scene is set by the commentator at the beginning: 'The match ends and to the delight of Norwich and to the horror of the police, Manchester United has lost for the first time in 15 games. The duel on the field may be over but as far as some of the visitors are concerned, the battle has only just begun.' Cue grainy images of young men leaving the stand, kicking at fences and running down steps. To chants of 'United', two young men are seen on the roof of a stand whilst missiles are being thrown at the helmeted police. In turn the police shove at the departing fans whilst emergency vehicle sirens can be heard in the distance. 'It's the worst riot ever seen in Norwich. With the Barclay Stand walls wrecked and the perimeter fences on fire, the Manchester United supporters are herded back to their trains and coaches.'[24]

A considerable number of middle-aged men have delighted in publishing books about their time in the various football 'squads' and gangs of the 1970s and 80s. I guess there is always a market for books about violence and toxic masculinity. Richard Kurt and Chris Nickeas' account of following Manchester United in the 1970s is certainly more entertaining than most. They describe the damage caused to Carrow Road and captured so vividly on the BBC's cameras as a 'nail in the coffin of the Red Army',[25] in that it was the riot after the Norwich game that led to the police, government and clubs getting their act together to challenge the disorder. 'Steve from Huddersfield' is quoted by Kurt and Nickeas describing the scene after the final whistle as 'like a film set scene, after a victorious army has sacked a small town'.[26] You know what, for a lad now attending the University of East Anglia in the 'fine city', it was simply terrifying.

23 Available at: https://www.mufcinfo.com/manupag/match_data/match_sql.php?my_match_date=1977-04-02 (accessed 14 May 2025).

24 Available at: https://www.youtube.com/watch?v=5ytRC9rnnwl (accessed 14 May 2025).

25 Kurt and Nickeas, *The Red Army Years*, p. 165.

26 Ibid., p. 166.

The Manchester United manager's response was as blunt as ever after the game. When asked what he'd like to see done to football hooligans, Tommy Docherty said, 'I'd like to try the birch, and take it from there, but the authorities are afraid to do this.'[27]

The Coming of the Commercial Manager

Norwich City's match against Liverpool on Saturday 20 March 1976 was the club's first sponsored match, with Dunlop Tyres no doubt attracted by Norwich's big city opponents. John Bond is quoted in the match programme as saying, 'I am delighted with the venture. At a time when money is so tight, we have to explore all avenues.'

The match programme for Norwich vs Manchester United, price 15 pence, provides a marvellous insight into the financial state of the game at this time as well as offering key information about the two teams on show. On page 17 of the programme there is a feature on a new appointment by Norwich City, a Mr Nigel Mackay, the club's first commercial manager. The club had announced the appointment on 22 March 1977, having recruited Mackay from Eastern Counties Newspapers, where he had been the marketing manager.[28]

Mackay is interviewed extensively in the programme piece discussing raising revenue for the club, including through sponsorship, advertising and a lottery. He speaks very presciently, saying, 'I don't think that anything I've mentioned will impinge on the actual football, because I sympathise with people who are a little bit frightened that commercial interests could spoil the game.' In 1977 neither Norwich City nor Manchester United were able to display any sponsors' brands on their kit, although the manufacturer's name, Admiral, was prominent both on United's famous red shirts and the Canaries' own yellow strip. The Norwich City keeper, Kevin Keelan, is pictured in the programme behind the wheel of a Renault 20, as free use of the car for a year was promised by the Reliance Garage (Heigham Street, Norwich) to the player who won the Reliance Entertainment Award. Finally, the match and programme were sponsored by Golden Wonder Snacks and Crisps, although their logo doesn't appear anywhere.

27 Jon Spurling, *Get It On: How the '70s Rocked Football* (Biteback Publishing, 2022), p. 304.

28 Woodrow, *Norwich City Football Club*, vol. II, 22 March 1977.

In John Bond's matchday column, the Norwich manager welcomes the appointment of Nigel Mackay and steps into the contemporary debate about shirt sponsorship by declaring his support for trade and brand names on the players' shirts. Bond also welcomed the representatives of Golden Wonder to the game, noting that the crisp company was looking into 'the best ways of linking their name responsibly with top class sport'. Meantime, following the violence after the game at Carrow Road in April 1977, Mackay would have had his work cut out trying to encourage brands to be associated with the sport as represented by some of its followers, and the coverage it received in the media.

Match day ticket

Author's collection

Racism and the Black Pioneers

It is hard to believe the sheer level of racism that black players were subject to in the 1970s and 80s. It was regular and systemic. It is important to read the autobiographies and biographies of those players who faced this, and, in Viv Anderson's words, 'overcame prejudice to achieve great things and change the face of British football forever'.[29] For the latter part of the 1970s, three black players at West Bromwich Albion, Brendan Batson, Laurie Cunningham and Cyrille Regis, lit up the English game with their flair and charisma, and they were collectively known in the English media as 'The Three Degrees', after the American female singing group. This was a time when racism blighted the game, when the fascist National Front organised on football terraces, and when some white fans chanted racist abuse (including 'monkey noises') to try to provoke and intimidate black players.

Laurie Cunningham was the first black player to sign for WBA in March 1977, with Cyrille Regis joining him just two months later in May. Regis described the abuse that Cunningham and he received from the Newcastle fans in a match in September 1997: 'There were monkey chants whenever we touched the ball. It would be commonplace over the next few seasons, but this was the first time I'd experienced it.'[30] Brendan Batson signed for Albion in 1978. He has also written of the volume of abuse that he and others faced at that time: 'That first game for Albion against Birmingham when I ran out of the tunnel and slipped. I looked down and saw I had stepped on a banana.'[31]

'The Three Degrees' were popular at West Bromwich Albion, but the racism that they and other people of colour faced across British society in the 1970s led to the Anti-Nazi League being set up, with branches in many cities, including Norwich. Badges from the era

Author's collection

29 Viv Anderson, 'Foreword', in Bill Hern and David Gleave, *Football's Black Pioneers* (Conker Editions, 2020), p. 8. Viv Anderson was the first black player to play for the England senior men's football team, being first selected in 1978.

30 Cyrille Regis, *Cyrille Regis – My Story* (André Deutsch, 2011), p. 77.

31 Brendon Batson, *The Third Degree: My Autobiography* (Curtis Sport, 2023), p. 171.

Welcome Fash

Justinus Soni Fashanu was not the first person of colour to represent Norwich City. That distinction belongs to Tony Collins, a left winger, who was signed from Watford for a fee of about £5,000 in 1953.[32] Collins went on to become the first black manager in the Football League at Rochdale and was present when Norwich defeated Rochdale in the League Cup Final of 1962. More recently, Johnny Miller had turned out for Norwich City between 1974 and 1976, having been signed from local rivals Ipswich Town. Miller was part of Norwich's Second Division promotion side in 1974/75 under John Bond.

Justin Fashanu ('Fash' as he was nicknamed) stood out immediately as much as for his stature and his upbringing as for his football. Justin was a fearless physical striker who had a reputation as a boxer as much as a footballer. He lost the British Schoolboy Heavyweight Final in March 1977 aged 16 years. Justin had grown up, along with his brother, John, as a fostered child (from the age of four years) in a white family, living in Shropham in the Norfolk countryside. As young players of colour, the Fashanu brothers had many more barriers than most to face and overcome in finding their place at Norwich City Football Club. Justin Fashanu became the youngest player to sign for Norwich as a full professional in December 1978. His first-team debut was against a West Bromwich Albion team including all three of Cyrille Regis, Brendan Batson and Laurie Cunningham, in January 1979. Justin's career was only just beginning.

Whilst the majority of Norwich fans loved Justin, a minority were still likely to abuse black players on other teams, and the National Front were active on the terraces at Carrow Road. In Jim Read's excellent biography of Fashanu, he tells a story of how the young player found himself in a pub at the same time as a National Front group who had been attending the racists' party conference in Great Yarmouth. Following some threats from the NF supporters, Fashanu broke the jaw of one of them.[33]

32 Hern and Gleave, *Football's Black Pioneers*.

33 Jim Read, *Justin Fashanu: The Biography* (DB Publishing, 2012).

Match Report: 9 February 1980, k/o 15:00. Football League Division One, Carrow Road, Norwich City 3 Liverpool 5. Attendance: 25,418.[34]

Norwich City
Kevin Keelan, Kevin Bond, Greg Downs, John Ryan, Roger Brown, David Jones, Peter Mendham (Mick McGuire), Kevin Reeves, Justin Fashanu, Graham Paddon, Martin Peters.
Manager: John Bond.

Liverpool
Ray Clemence, Phil Neal, Alan Kennedy, Phil Thompson, Ray Kennedy, Alan Hansen, Kenny Dalglish, Jimmy Case, David Fairclough, Terry McDermott, Sammy Lee. Manager: Bob Paisley.

Goals
Norwich City: Peters (1), Reeves (37), Fashanu (81)
Liverpool: Fairclough (4, 18, 75), Dalglish (88), Case (89)

As Rob Hadgraft accurately notes, Norwich City fans of a certain age (including myself) remember Justin Fashanu's finest hour all too well.[35] *It came in one of the most exciting games I have ever been to. Even though the Canaries lost!*

The Liverpool team that arrived in Norwich towards the end of the 1979/80 season, managed by Bob Paisley, was awash with international players, including Ray Clemence, Phil Neal, Phil Thompson, Ray Kennedy, Alan Hansen, Jimmy Case and Kenny Dalglish. This was in Liverpool's pomp. The club won eleven League titles and four European Cups in the 1970s and 80s. Paisley's team had won the First Division title in 1978/79 and were top at the time Norwich played them (Liverpool went on to win the title – one of their seven successes in the First Division in the 1980s). Norwich meanwhile were in ninth position, but only eight points behind the league leaders. Norwich had just lost an FA Cup replay against Wolves 2–3 at home, and after a pulsating 3–3 draw with Ipswich Town on Boxing Day, the largest crowd of the season at Carrow Road (25,624) would have been hoping to see some goals. Hopefully not all scored by Liverpool, who had beaten Norwich 6–0 at Anfield the year previously. Kevin Reeves was Norwich's top goalscorer at this

34 A more complete match report can be found in Edward Couzens-Lake, *Greatest Games: Norwich City* (Pitch Publishing, 2012), pp. 72–5.

35 Rob Hadgraft, *Norwich City: The Modern Era. A Complete Record* (Desert Island Books, 2003).

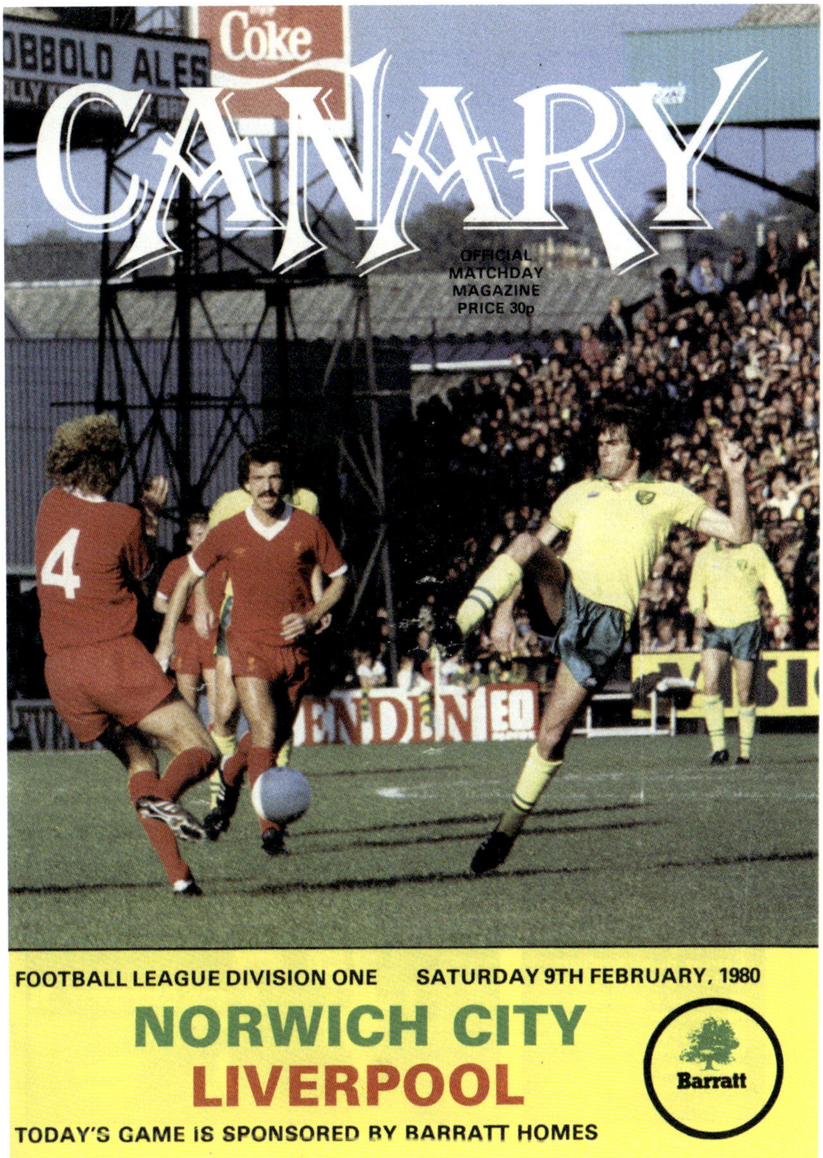

The cover of the match programme for Norwich City vs Liverpool, 9 February 1980

Author's collection

time of the season with nine, but young Justin Fashanu was only one behind having scored eight. Meantime, commercial manager 'Mac' Mackay was doing his business in the match programme, looking for match sponsors such as Barratt Homes, who were the sponsors of the Liverpool game.

This was a match which started with a bang and finished in breathless style. Norwich opened the scoring that Saturday afternoon, with Martin Peters scoring a header as early as the second minute. Perennial Liverpool super sub David Fairclough (although he actually started this game) replied with two quick goals before Kevin Reeves equalised to make it a half-time score of 2–2. Fairclough then scored again for his first and only senior hat-trick to make it 2–3 after 75 minutes. The last 15 minutes of the match were electrifying. In the 81st minute, Justin Fashanu scored the goal that made 'Goal of the Season' on BBC's Match of the Day. You can still find it today on YouTube. Fashanu received the ball with his back to goal, just outside the penalty box. With a flick from his right foot, he turned and volleyed with his left foot into the far top corner of Clemence's goal to make the score 3–3. It was a sensational strike and was undoubtedly the best goal of Fashanu's career. Even his celebration was cool, turning and simply lifting his right arm with an impassive look on his face, making the moment iconic. Sadly, the match didn't end there, and two predatory goals by Dalglish and Case in the 88th and 89th minutes brought Liverpool a famous 5–3 win.

Although I was of course disappointed by the late Liverpool goals, I was nevertheless well aware that I had witnessed a very special game. Fashanu's strike had huge impact. As Jim Read wrote, 'What made is so memorable was the element of surprise. No one on the pitch or in the stands saw it coming.'[36] It is a goal that gets replayed time after time and still appears in historical clips from Match of the Day.

It was Fashanu's goal against Liverpool, as well as his performances in the 1979/80 season with 11 goals (13 across all competitions), finishing as Norwich's top scorer, which brought the striker to the attention of Nottingham Forest's Brian Clough and Peter Taylor.

36 Read, *Justin Fashanu*, p. 31.

The End of an Era

Gerry Harrison, the Anglia TV commentator, described the 1970s as 'the decade when Norwich City took a giant step forward'.[37] It was a period when Norwich broke into the big time of English football, reaching Wembley for the first time and with two cup finals along the way. The decade ended symbolically for the club with the demolition of the old River End terrace next to the River Wensum, which was replaced by a new two-tiered £1.25 million construction, the River End Stand, in December 1979, complete with an exclusive '101' club with dining facilities for 101 season ticket holders[38] and a new public house at the rear, The Nest, which opened in April 1980 – reportedly the first on the premises of a football ground.[39] The future looked bright.

It was the decade in which colour television and increasing broadcast figures enabled those in the football business to see how money could be made and how they could better exploit their sport. Liverpool's shirt sponsorship with the Japanese company Hitachi commenced at the start of the 1979/80 season; Norwich would wait until 1983 for their first commercial hook-up of this kind.

The task facing Norwich City's new commercial manager was clear to see, even when the game was full of larger-than-life characters who knew how to entertain. Whilst older football fans might be fond of reminiscing about the days when the game seemed to be simpler, it was also wracked by racism and violence. Norwich's Justin Fashanu would face new challenges in the 1980s when he moved to Nottingham Forest under Brian Clough, not only because of his skin colour, but also because of his sexuality. For many, football seemed to be blighted, attracting opprobrium from many in the political and moral establishment and making it a hard commercial sell to companies outside the usual alcohol and cigarette advertisers targeting the sport's majority young, male, working-class audience.

Margaret Thatcher's election in May 1979 would have a huge impact on football, as her economic policies encouraged free market capitalism at all costs. The commercial exploitation of the nation's assets, with increased profits for those entrepreneurs able to join her on her journey, were at the top of her plans to transform society. And whilst Thatcher had no interest in sport, she certainly had her eyes on football.

37 Gerry Harrison, 'Foreword', in Edward Couzens-Lake, *Norwich City: The Seventies* (Amberley Publishing, 2013), p. 9.

38 Woodrow, *Norwich City Football Club*, vol. III, 19 July 1979.

39 Ibid., vol. III, 25 April 1980.

adidas

THE 1980s

Football's Dark Decade

Football's Dark Decade

1981	'Ghost Town' released by The Specials in June; Toxteth riots
1982	The Falklands War; Channel 4 launches in November
1983	Tottenham Hotspur floats on the stock market, avoiding the FA's restrictions on dividends and enabling football clubs to be profit-making vehicles for investors; Shirt sponsorship is permitted by the BBC for televised games; Clubs stop sharing gate receipts
1984	Battle of Orgreave, 18 June, part of the 1984–85 UK miners' strike; The Los Angeles Olympics, July–August, an event built on television and commercial sponsorship.
1985	Crowd trouble shown on television at the Luton vs Millwall FA Cup quarter-final; Bradford fire, 11 May: 56 fans die; Fan violence at the European Cup Final (29 May) between Liverpool and Juventus at the Heysel Stadium in Brussels: 39 people die; English football clubs are banned from European competition from 1985 until 1990; Riots across Handsworth, Brixton, Toxteth and Broadwater Farm, September–October
1986	Popplewell Inquiry
1987	Play-offs introduced to the English Football League
1989	Hillsborough disaster, 15 April: 97 fans die; Fall of the Berlin Wall, 9 November

Previous spread: Norwich City's Adidas strip worn between 1981 and 1983 (replica). Background: the cover of the match programme for Norwich City vs Leicester City, 21 April 1983

Author's collections

Free Market Football in Rundown Stadiums

Margaret Thatcher's election in 1979 marked a seismic change in British society. The new government embraced free market capitalism with no brakes attached. Where previous governments had bailed out failing industries such as car manufacturing, the new Conservative government was content to let them go to the wall, allowing unemployment figures to reach unprecedented highs. Following the energy crises of the preceding decade, Thatcher was prepared to take on the miners' unions using the police to win violent confrontations across the coalfields of South Yorkshire. The Falklands (Malvinas) War even allowed some flag-waving, albeit at the cost of Argentinian and British lives. There was discontent and sporadic rioting throughout the decade in many of England's most disadvantaged inner-city areas. Some of those on the streets were protesting against the presence of far-right groups and the perceived racism of the police.

Thatcher was clearly not interested in football; indeed, 'The sporting world was one she did not understand and did not want to understand.'[1] However, football fans were not dissimilar to striking trade unionists on her agenda. The football violence of the 1970s and 80s was followed by the disasters and tragedies of 1985 and then Hillsborough in 1989. The Conservative government clearly saw these as 'law and order' issues and initially legislated for football supporter ID cards under the Football Spectators Act of 1989.

Thatcher's laissez-faire approach to free markets encouraged football club owners to seek new ways of making their own businesses more profitable. Barriers were removed to the profits that could be made in football, mirroring the changes in the sport that had enabled coaches to look to continental Europe to try to exploit cheaper sources of labour and identify players who might fit into English football. As we shall see, the BBC's removal of its restrictions on shirt advertising in the games it broadcast meant that sponsors could move in to exploit the marketing opportunities enabled by having their brand placed on players' shirts and in front of the television camera.

In 1985 a fire in a wooden stand at Bradford City caused 56 deaths. Just eighteen days later, the Heysel Stadium disaster at another very dilapidated ground at the 1985 European Cup Final between Liverpool and Juventus marked the beginning of the huge changes which were to

1 Ian Herbert, *The Independent*, 9 April 2013.

take place in football in England. To begin with, UEFA banned English clubs from taking part in its competitions from 1985 to 1990. Following the deaths of 97 spectators at Hillsborough in 1989, the sport had to change simply to survive.[2]

The fall of the Berlin Wall in November 1989 symbolised in many ways the victory of free-market capitalism. As football was developing as a global industry, it was affected by powerful non-economic factors, as were all other economic sectors.[3] The end of the Cold War in Europe heralded a huge change in European football, including English football, as we shall see in the following chapter.

As with all English football clubs in the 1980s, therefore, it was a turbulent decade for Norwich City.

Player cards (Figurine Panini, Football 81 & 78).

The 1980 departures of Kevin Reeves (March) and manager John Bond (October) to Manchester City were both critical.

Author's collection

'The crazy years' – When Transfer Fees Took Off

In *Back Page Football*, Stephen Kelly writes that the transfer of 22-year-old striker Kevin Reeves from Norwich City to Manchester City for £1.25 million in March 1980 was part of 'The crazy years when transfer fees went through the ceiling.'[4] He laid the blame for this rapid inflation on the clubs' respective managers, John Bond and Malcolm Allison.

John Bond had worked hard at Norwich on a limited budget and had signed Reeves from Bournemouth (Bond's own former club) for £50,000, with the young striker making his debut against Arsenal in January 1977. Reeves, whilst never prolific, proved to be a regular scorer and, in particular, he formed a productive and popular partnership with Justin Fashanu following Fashanu's debut in January 1979. Reeves even won an England senior cap whilst still at Norwich, against Bulgaria in November 1979. When the bid came for Reeves, it proved impossible for chairman Sir Arthur South or Bond to resist. This was big money to a club like Norwich City – in fact it was big money to most clubs. It wasn't the first £1 million transfer; that had come a year earlier when Trevor Francis moved from Birmingham City to Nottingham Forest. But it was Norwich's first. Not that it excited the fans to make over £1 million profit on Reeves; as a famous banner put it at the time, 'No Reeves, no fans, no future!'[5]

2 The number of fatalities was adjusted to 97 following the death of Liverpool supporter Andrew Devine in 2021, as a result of suffering severe and irreversible brain damage at Hillsborough.

3 Antonio Missiroli, 'European football cultures and their integration: the "short" twentieth century', *Sport in Society*, 5.1 (2002): 1-20.

4 Stephen F. Kelly, *Back Page Football: A Century of Newspaper Coverage* (Queen Anne Press, 1988), p. 182.

5 Rick Waghorn, *Canary Greats* (Jarrold Publishing and Norwich City Football Club, 2004), p. 111.

Norwich, then, were establishing themselves as a 'selling' club. It probably didn't help to mollify the fans that Reeves' sale helped to finance a new stand to replace the River End terrace, the last open side of the Carrow Road ground. This ensured that there was covered accommodation around the ground and fulfilled the safety regulations of the time.

Dražen Mužinić's Milkman

Player card (Figurine Panini, Argentina 78 World Cup)

Author's collection

Brian Clough had won the league in 1978 with an entirely British side, and in later life he said, 'I would have problems with the foreign players because they wouldn't be able to understand me and I certainly can't speak half of their languages.'[6] Between 1931 and 1978, the FA had effectively banned overseas footballers from playing in England through a two-year residency rule to deter imports.[7] But the FA, under pressure from the European Economic Community, agreed to a maximum of two foreign players per club from the summer of 1978. New opportunities for bringing in new talent – and not only from Europe – were immediately identified by some clubs and managers. Tottenham were first off the mark after Argentina won the FIFA World Cup in 1978. The charismatic Osvaldo (Ossie) Ardiles and Ricardo (Ricky) Villa were recruited from Huracán (Buenos Aires) and Racing Avallenda respectively into the Spurs midfield. Villa's spectacular winning goal against Manchester City in the 1981 FA Cup Final replay is still remembered (and watched). Other overseas imports into British football at this time included Alberto Tarantini (Birmingham City) and Ivan Golac (Southampton), and Ipswich Town's influential Dutch players, Arnold Műhren and Frans Thijssen.

Following the loss of Kevin Reeves and then Martin Peters, who left to be player manager at Sheffield United in July 1980, Bond was no doubt looking for ways to spend his money wisely and decided to look abroad for his next buy. An agreement to sign Dražen Mužinić, a Yugoslavian international, from Hajduk Split was made in August 1980. This was a transfer from continental Europe that really did not work out, even if a club record fee of £300,000 was paid for Mužinić (a Norwich City record that stood for another seven years). So began a story for Norwich City that many clubs and fans would share and understand over the years: the 'exotic' and expensive foreign transfer which promises so much ... before a ball has been kicked.

6 Available at: https://www.youtube.com/watch?v=gD-LlghOKXU (accessed 14 May 2025).

7 Nick Harris, *The Foreign Revolution: How Overseas Footballers Changed the English Game* (Aurum, 2006).

In his two years at Norwich Mužinić made 17 starts. He seemed to have Brian Clough's 'flair' for languages, as Norwich had to hire an interpreter from the University of East Anglia to help with communication. Unfortunately, no attempts to fit the Yugoslav into the club's playing style worked. Justin Fashanu has been widely reported as saying, 'I don't think we ever got Mužinić, I reckon they sent his milkman.'[8]

It would be ever thus. Thirty-three years later, Norwich City signed Dutch striker Ricky van Wolfswinkel in a transfer worth a reported £8.5 million. It was, like Mužinić, a lot of money for Norwich to spend on one player at that time. Van Wolfswinkel scored on his debut ... and then never again in the Premier League. Just a season later, he was loaned to Saint Etienne, then Real Betis, and finally sold to his first club, Vitesse, for an estimated €600,000 in 2016. It was a disastrous transfer for the Norfolk club.

Both Mužinić and van Wolfswinkel are reminders of the growing importance of money in football which began in the 1980s – not just in terms of how much you have, but how you spend it. Perhaps Mužinić's poor showing at Norwich, together with frustrations over how much money was made available for transfers, helped to encourage John Bond in seeking pastures new. Just six months after Kevin Reeves had left Norwich for Manchester City, John Bond made the same journey in October 1980 (Mužinić himself did not leave until June 1982). The problem of building a competitive team was left with Ken Brown, Bond's deputy, and now the new manager of Norwich City.

The Tragic Story of Justin Fashanu

Ken Brown made some major signings when he took over, including Dave Watson (eventually Norwich's third £1 million sale when he returned to Everton in 1986) and Northern Ireland international Martin O'Neill. Unfortunately, Brown was unable to keep City in the First Division and O'Neill left after one season for a fee of £300,000 to Manchester City (again!). Goalkeeper Chris Woods had originally come on loan from Queens Park Rangers, but signed permanently for £225,000 at the beginning of the 1981/82 season. Justin Fashanu also moved at the beginning of the season in August 1981, a move which turned out to be disastrous for all concerned.

8 Mike Davage, *Glorious Canaries, Past and Present, 1902–1994* (Norwich City Football Club, 1994), p. 270.

Player card: (Topps Chewing Gum)
Author's collection

When Forest bid £1 million and secured the transfer of Fashanu from Norwich, it marked a significant and exciting step upwards for the 20-year-old. Of course, the Forest fans still love Clough, and he remains a giant in the mythology of the game. But along with his successes at first Derby County and then at Nottingham Forest following brief but unsuccessful spells at Brighton and Leeds, Clough was also known for his autocratic style and his abrasive and often controversial views.

When Fashanu arrived at Forest's City Ground, next to the River Trent, the young striker came with a reputation, not only for his football but for an increasingly flamboyant lifestyle, together with a growing religious conviction, neither of which were likely to find favour with his outspoken and blunt new manager. Clough had failed at Leeds United where he alienated leading players such as Norman Hunter and Johnny Giles. Fashanu's liking for flashy cars and disregard for paying his parking fines was never going to go down well with a manager who is remembered for wanting his players to do what they were told. The striker's time with Forest was a failure for both club and player, with Clough describing the million-pound fee as the worst money Forest had ever invested and blaming Peter Taylor for the signing.

However, it is another side of Justin Fashanu that he is most remembered for, and Clough writes about this in his autobiography. Fashanu had become a regular visitor to gay clubs in Nottingham and he was clearly coming to terms with his homosexuality. It was not easy being gay in Britain in the 1980s, and it must have been even harder being a young, gay, black man, who held evangelical Christian views in addition. Fashanu was always an outsider at Forest, and part of this was no doubt related to his sexuality and the aggressive masculinity of the English game at this time. Clough's description of his relationship with Fashanu has not worn well and reflects football's long battle with homophobia. As Clough related, much of the publicity around his young signing centred on Fashanu's private life. Clough wrote, when describing Fashanu's visits to gay clubs, 'I presume he's still visiting the same places when he's in need of a loaf of bread.'[9] Fashanu also had his own approach to keeping healthy and fit, and when he came to training with his own masseur, Clough had had enough. He ordered Fashanu to leave the training ground and called on the Nottingham police to have the player removed.

9 Brian Clough (with John Sadler), *Clough: The Autobiography* (Partridge Press, 1994), p. 233.

At this same time, Fashanu was dealing with more intrusions into his private life, with the *Sunday People* newspaper running a story about the rumours about his sexuality. Still aged only 21, Fashanu dealt with the allegations with an emphatic denial: 'I am not gay.' Frank Clark, who managed Fashanu later, was much more understanding and sympathetic than Clark's former manager at Forest, as Clark relates in his own autobiography. Fashanu was terrified about coming out publicly, although Clark and the club's physio knew he was gay and supported him. In October 1990 *The Sun* ran a new story, '£1m Soccer Star: I Am Gay', including an interview with the footballer.

Fashanu was sold to Notts County in December 1982 for £150,000. Not a good return on Britain's first million-pound black player. From this stage on, Fashanu's football career went into freefall. He was all too often the centre of fan and media attention whilst dealing with ongoing problems with injuries and fitness. He officially retired from the professional game in 1997. On 3 May 1998, following an allegation of sexual assault on a young man in the US (which Fashanu denied), Justin Fashanu died by suicide at the age of 37 years. Homophobic behaviour is still common, particularly on social media platforms, and Fashanu was the first elite footballer to identify as gay in British football. It wasn't until 2022 that Jake Daniels at Blackpool became the first openly gay English professional footballer since Fashanu. And it hasn't been easy for Daniels either; he has spent the subsequent years on loan at amateur Northern Premier League sides.[10]

As for Fashanu, he was inducted into Norwich City's Hall of Fame in February 2010 and into the National Football Museum's Hall of Fame in 2020. After Martin Peters, he is the only other Norwich City player to have received this honour.

Football in Dividends

In the 1970s most clubs' income still came from matchday ticket sales, and it is easy to see why clubs appointed commercial managers to maximise any additional opportunities for income they could find. Football's administrators and its leading clubs had already been seeking ways of making more money from the game, which had originally been established by the Football League on a system of shared gate money; thus the bigger

10 Amos Wynn, *Blackpool Gazette*, 7 February 2024. Available at: https://www.blackpoolgazette.co.uk/sport/football/blackpool-fc/ive-learnt-to-carry-on-day-to-day-blackpools-jake-daniels-discusses-blocking-out-hate-and-receiving-support-from-an-olympian-4508300 (accessed 14 May 2025).

clubs supported those less able to attract larger crowds of spectators. The FA had established restrictions against unlimited dividends in 1892 to prevent what it saw as 'the dangers of commercialism',[11] and these rules had stayed in place until the 1980s. Thatcher's government had deregulated financial transactions and relaxed lending criteria, and as part of her drive towards the privatisation of public industries such as the utility companies, she prioritised shareholders before the state's interests.[12] Irving Scholar was no doubt a fan of these new approaches to business, and football was certainly ripe for change. As a Tottenham Hotspur fan and property owner, albeit then domiciled in Monte Carlo, Scholar forced himself on to the board at Tottenham and immediately sought to circumvent Football League rules. In 1983 the directors of Tottenham Hotspur floated the club on the stock market, thus avoiding the FA's restrictions on dividends and enabling the club to become a profit-making vehicle for investors. This led to the resignation of the manager Keith Burtenshaw, due to 'the growing corporate influence at the club'.[13] It was also in 1983 that clubs stopped sharing gate receipts from match attendances.

The seat price at Carrow Road increased in three years from £3.00 to £5.50 ...

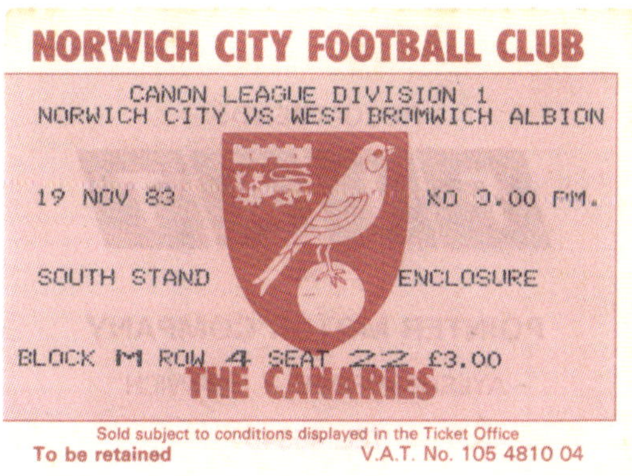

Two match tickets in the 1980s. The seat price at Carrow Road increased in three years from £3.00 to £5.50 although they may be in different stands. Norwich City's admission prices in 1980/81 included a rise in seat prices from £2.40 to £3.00 and from £2.85 to £3.50.[14]

Author's collection

11 David Conn, *The Beautiful Game? Searching for the Soul of Football* (Yellow Jersey Press, 2005), p. 42.

12 Roger Domeneghetti, *Everybody Wants to Rule the World: Britain, Sport & the 1980s* (Vintage, 2024).

13 Ibid., p. 337.

14 James Woodrow (as compiled for the Norwich City Football Club), *Norwich City Football Club: The Archive* (Severn, 2022), vol. III, 15 May 1980.

Television was changing as well. At the beginning of the 1980s there were still only three channels – BBC1, BBC2 and ITV. The Football League had historically not allowed live football coverage until after half-time, in case fans were encouraged to watch the game in front of their television sets rather than turning up to a ground and paying an entrance fee.

At this same time, sports sponsorship was growing rapidly as sports such as darts, snooker and cricket found new television audiences. The sponsorship was totally unregulated, and 'many governing bodies of sport feared they would be over-run with commercialism'.[15] In 1981 the Central Council of Physical Recreation established a Committee of Inquiry into sports sponsorship, with Denis Howell, a former Minister of Sport, as its chair. The Howell Report was published in 1983[16] and included a chapter on 'Ethical Considerations'. In referencing alcohol, gambling and tobacco sponsorship, it concluded that as these products were lawful, they 'must also be presumed to come within the ambit of personal choice and personal freedom'.[17] This sentiment certainly reflected the ideology of the government of the time and will have pleased the bosses of these industries. Despite this, the report still raised concerns about the importance of sport in society and the commercial standards relating to how it operated.

Meantime, on the other side of the Atlantic, the Los Angeles Olympics of 1984 were based on commodifying and sponsoring as many aspects of the games as possible. The American model of sponsorship and sale of television rights, accompanied by the latest technology to show all aspects of the match and game action on your screen, was a gamechanger, showing that the smart marketing of sport could yield a profit. Sport had always been an entertainment product; now there were more opportunities to market it to consumers.[18] The LA Olympics, along with the commercial and exciting packaging of American football on the new Channel 4 television channel, helped Scholar and others such as David Dein at Arsenal to appreciate the critical role that broadcasting, and the sale of TV rights, would play then and in the future. Already in 1985 there were discussions led by the 'big clubs' to form a breakaway league that could attract its own television deals. The Football League headed this off with concessions,

15 Denis Howell, *Made in Birmingham: The Memoirs of Denis Howell* (Macdonald Queen Anne Press, 1990), p. 347.

16 The Central Council for Physical Recreation, *Committee of Enquiry into Sports Sponsorship: "The Howell Report"* (The Central Council for Physical Recreation, 1983).

17 Ibid., p. 93.

18 Robin Ireland, *Sport, Sponsorship and Public Health* (Routledge, 2023).

including an agreement that a higher percentage of TV and sponsorship money would go to the clubs in the First Division.

Branded Shirts

Attendances at Football League grounds fell from a peak of 41.3 million in 1948/49 to 18.4 million in 1983/84. Records were being broken, but not in a good way. When Norwich City won 2–0 at Everton on Saturday 11 April 1981 (with goals from Royle and Fashanu), the crowd of 16,254 was the Merseyside club's lowest since the Second World War.[19] Similarly, West Bromwich Albion's attendance of 9,189 when they hosted the Canaries on Saturday 2 May 1983 was their lowest in twenty-six years.[20]

The Norwich City Football Club Archive includes an annual report and financial statement for the year to 30 June 1981. The club's £1,609,626 income includes gate receipts and receipts from cup pools of £885,280, and a commercial income of £676,949, of which £72,807 came from advertising and sponsorship.[21]

As matchday income was critical to club income at this time, the Football League invited Sir Norman Chester, who had led a similar inquiry in 1968, to review the game once again in response to what was seen as a long-term decline in paying customers attending professional football in England. The Chester Report was published in 1983. As seems to be standard for any independent review of football by an outside body, the Football League clubs rejected the majority of the Chester Committee's recommendations, which included, for example, replacing the then Division Three and Division Four with three geographically based leagues of 18 teams. The Chester Committee noted a lack of commercial awareness among clubs, which resulted in them not being able to maximise revenues, and highlighted the slow development of sponsorship, for example. This was in contrast to the United States, where sport was developing as an entertainment activity, and where the National Football League signed a five-year television contract worth $2000 million in 1982.

The Chester Report made various recommendations, including that 'clubs adopt a new customer orientation. To this end, the League should commission and finance, from sponsorship revenues, market research and other marketing activities, including advertising.'[22] It recommended

19 Woodrow, *Norwich City Football Club*, vol. III, 11 April 1981.

20 Ibid., vol. III, 2 May 1983.

21 Ibid., vol. III, 26 August 1981.

22 Football League, *Report of the Committee of Enquiry into Structure and Finance* (Chairman, Sir Norman Chester) (Football League, 1983).

that the practice of sharing television rights equally amongst all League clubs should be discontinued. It was already being noted by some commentators that an imbalance of sponsorship income might consolidate the dominance of already wealthy and successful clubs. The report also noted the risk that some of the top clubs might be tempted to form a 'super-league' of breakaway clubs.

An original Poll Withey sponsored shirt, which has seen better days.
Collection of Alan Ward

Colin Benson was the editor of *Canary*, Norwich City's matchday programme, at the start of the 1983/84 season.[23] He described the meeting of the League club chairmen which took place in July 1983 and approved a broadcasting deal which allowed the Milk Cup Final (the League Cup was sponsored by the Milk Marketing Board and then Milk Marketing Ltd, from 1981 to 1986) to be screened live on a Sunday, together with ten League games and some FA Cup matches. Importantly, the broadcasting agreement also allowed shirt advertisements to be shown. Benson complained that the arrangement strongly favoured the big clubs which had arrangements for shirt sponsorship already in place. In this same season (1983/84), the top division became the Canon League, Division One, reflecting the new sponsorship deal.

Adidas replaced Admiral as Norwich City's kit supplier in 1981, and its stylish yellow shirt with narrow green vertical pinstripes was worn for three seasons. The BBC had refused to show matches featuring teams with shirt sponsors initially, and it wasn't until the July 1983 broadcasting deal with the Football League that this situation changed; by 1987 all English professional teams had a shirt sponsor. Norwich City's own shirt advertiser and sponsorship deal was announced in the match programme for the game against Leicester City by the commercial manager, Nigel Mackay. Mackay had come a long way since the game against Manchester United in April 1977. He described the new sponsorship deal as a key milestone in Norwich's history, up there with the move from an amateur to a professional club, to the adoption of green and yellow as the club colours, and the moves to new and better stadiums. The Adidas logo and embroidered club badge were now joined by a commercial brand below them for the first time.

The three-year contract with a double-glazing company, Poll and Withey Windows Ltd, was worth £150,000. The sponsorship agreement allowed

23 Colin Benson, 'Benno at Large', *Canary*, 31 August 1983.

POLL
WITHEY

the company's logo to appear in red on the front of the players' shirts.[24] The value of the deal can be contrasted with the £500,000 three-year agreement between JVC (a Japanese electronics giant) and Arsenal which was signed in 1981. The Thetford-based glass company seems to have been dissolved in 1994 (that was when its last accounts were filed at Companies House), but the company directors at least had the satisfaction of being on the front of City's shirts when they beat Sunderland in the Milk Cup Final at Wembley in March 1985.

Poll and Withey was the first of many companies with a Norfolk connection to be Norwich City's shirt sponsor. The value of the sponsorship, of course, would always be linked to the size of the club's marketing reach. And even with the advent of the Premier League, Norwich City's support would continue to be rooted in the county.

Sponsorship has always been more than simply placing an advertisement, and even in these early days, companies looked for player endorsements, like that by Norwich City goalkeeper Chris Woods, right. Some players have always pushed back, however, against being obliged to promote brands and products that they do not want to be associated with. When Laurie Cunningham arrived at Real Madrid following his transfer from West Bromwich Albion, he was approached with a rush of offers from Pepsi-Cola, a shaving cream and a television manufacturer. He rejected them all saying, 'I could never be commercialised like Kevin Keegan, I am not into that and I don't want to be, though there's no doubt you can make more money outside the game than in it.'[25] Kevin Keegan in his time at Hamburg between 1977 and 1980 – having helped them to become Bundesliga champions in 1978/79 – was receiving £125,000 a year from BP and was advertising milk on German television. In Jon Spurling's excellent review of English football in the 1980s, he quotes Keegan's Hamburg striking partner Horst Hrubesch as saying, 'Kevin is as comfortable in a business suit as a football kit.'[26] Keegan captained the England team on 31 occasions including at the UEFA Euros in 1980, and it could be argued that he recognised very early both the future direction football was taking and the resulting commercial potential for himself.

24 Woodrow, *Norwich City Football Club*, vol. III, 18 October 1983.

25 Ronald Atkin talking to Laurie Cunningham in *The Observer*, quoted in *Canary*, match programme for Norwich City vs Liverpool, 9 February 1980.

26 Jon Spurling, *Go To War: Football on the Brink in the 80s* (Biteback Publishing, 2024), p. 8.

Advertisement in the match programme of Norwich City vs QPR, 29 October 1983. Chris Woods is behind the wheel of a Fiat provided by the Pointer Motor Company of Norwich, the match sponsor

Author's collection

Advertisement on the front inside cover of the match programme for Norwich City vs Stoke City, 21st April 1984

Author's collection

Match Report: Wednesday 19 October 1983, k/o 19:30.
Canon League Division One, Carrow Road, Norwich City 3 Leicester City 1.
Attendance: 13,780.

Norwich City
Chris Woods, Paul Haylock, Greg Downs, Peter Mendham, Åge Hareide, Dave Watson, Louie Donowa, Mike Channon, John Devine, Keith Bertschin, Dave Bennett. Manager: Ken Brown.

Leicester City
Mark Wallington, Tommy Williams, Ian Wilson, Kevin MacDonald, Bob Hazel, Ian Banks, Steve Lynex, Gary Lineker, Peter Eastoe, Paul Ramsey, Tom English. Manager: Gordon Milne.

Goals
Norwich City: Donowa (45), Bertschin (61), Channon (pen., 82)
Leicester City: Eastoe (31)

The match between Norwich City and Leicester City at Carrow Road early in the 1983/84 season is unlikely to be remembered long for its football. Although there were four goals, it was a fairly mundane fixture between two sides which ended the season next to each other with the same number of points (51) in 14th and 15th places in what was now the Canon League Division One. Norwich's superior goal difference (–1) secured them the higher position. But the match was certainly a major landmark in the Canaries' own story in the commercialisation of football, as it was the first time the Norwich City players wore sponsored shirts, as described previously.

Neither side had started their campaign well, with Norwich in 15th place and Leicester bottom of the pile in 22nd, with a single point. Norwich had only won twice all season, although they had picked up a 3–1 victory at Watford the preceding Saturday. The Leicester team included a 22-year-old striker called Gary Lineker, who was destined to go on to greater things. Norwich had Chris Woods in goal – an ever present along with Greg Downs that season – and a Norwegian sweeper, Åge Hareide, playing in defence. Times may have changed a bit for the modern footballer, as Ken Brown notes in the match programme that the club was seeking a furnished house for Hareide ('If you know of one that might be suitable please give me a ring'). Not sure that Manchester City's own Norwegian import in 2022, Erling Haaland, would have been advertising in the match programme for assistance.

Dave Watson was Norwich City captain in 1983/84 and in the centre of the defence. Both Watson and Woods received England call-ups that season. With the exception of Irish international John Devine, the rest of the home team were English. The old warhorse, 34-year-old Mick Channon, was up front for Norwich alongside Keith Bertschin.

In the event, the match reflected the clubs' league positions, despite the first goal coming from Leicester's Peter Eastoe from a long-distance shot. A young Louie Donowa equalised with a header just before half-time. Donowa remains one of the few players who have played for both Norwich and Ipswich. Bertschin scored the equaliser on his 100th appearance for the club and then was impeded late in the match, leading to a penalty. As Leicester City goalkeeper Mark Wallington dived to the right, the ever reliable Mick Channon tucked his shot away in the opposite corner, Norwich finishing as convincing 3–1 winners.

The cover of the match programme for Norwich City vs Leicester City, 21 April 1983, with the name of the new sponsor in the bottom right-hand corner

Author's collection

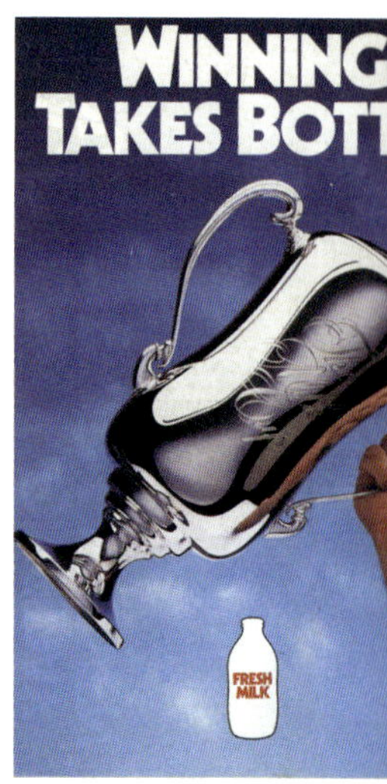

The front and back cover of the match programme for the Milk Cup Final, Norwich City vs Sunderland, 24 March 1985

Author's collection

Player card
(Panini, Football 87)
Author's collection

Match Report: Sunday 24 March 1985, k/o 14:00.
Milk Cup Final, Wembley Stadium, Norwich City 1 Sunderland 0.
Attendance: 100,000.

Norwich City
Chris Woods, Paul Haylock, Dennis Van Wijk, Steve Bruce, Peter Mendham, Dave Watson, Mark Barham, Mick Channon, John Deehan, Asa Hartford, Louie Donowa. Manager: Ken Brown.

Sunderland
Chris Turner, Barry Venison, Nick Pickering, Gary Bennett, Gordon Chisholm, David Corner (Howard Gayle), Peter Daniel, Ian Wallace, David Hodgson, Steve Berry, Clive Walker.
Manager: Len Ashurst.

Goals
Norwich City: Chisholm (o.g., 46)

The League Cup was first held in 1960/61, with Norwich City appearing in its second iteration in 1962, which the club won. They had also reached the final in 1973 and 1975, losing both matches 0–1. The League Cup Final was celebrating its Silver Jubilee in 1985. Alan Hardaker, the Football League secretary when the competition was launched, is quoted in the Norwich City vs Sunderland final match programme: 'I saw the League Cup simply as a fresh source of income for the clubs and a new source of entertainment for the fans.' The League Cup Final was first staged at Wembley in 1967, but it was the injection of sponsorship money that started to generate more serious revenue.

The National Dairy Council was the first title sponsor of the cup, and it was known as the Milk Cup between 1981 and 1986. The sponsorship money was £490,000 in 1985, but there were many other ancillary benefits to be derived, including television fees and advertising revenue. Importantly, winning the League Cup provided an entry into the UEFA Cup. I was one of the many thousands who were lucky enough to watch the match on television.

Norwich had scored plenty of goals on the way to Wembley in 1985: nine goals across two ties against Preston North End in September (with six different goalscorers), four in an away replay at Aldershot in November, and three more in a home fifth round win against Notts County later the same month. The semi-final had brought even more joy, as Norwich beat Ipswich Town by an aggregate score of 2–1, with a young Steve Bruce scoring the winner with a trademark bullet header with just minutes left. As Ken Brown recalls, for those Norwich City fans who were lucky enough to be present at the second leg under the floodlights at Carrow Road, this would be one of their all-time favourite matches and, in many ways, better than the final.[27]

The final at Wembley would not only provide the winners with a big silver cup to show off, it would also open the door to European competition. This was Norwich's third League Cup Final in thirteen years and, despite losing the previous two, they were still confident this time round. I liked hearing that Ken Brown tried to make sure the team didn't freeze at Wembley as they had in 1973 and 1975 by singing the same song over and over again on the coach on the way to the stadium: 'It's Now Or Never'.[28] *But there was plenty of experience in the team: Chris Woods, Asa Hartford, England defender and City captain Dave Watson, and veteran striker Mick Channon had all played at Wembley before. Just a week before, Norwich had lost 3–1 at home to Sunderland in the league, but no one read too much into that.*

Player card (Canary Collectables, 2001–02)

Author's collection

Like any other team who had made it this far, Norwich City were doing their best to get as much commercial benefit from the occasion as possible. City midfielder and King's Lynn-born Peter Mendham recalls the interest from local businesses, including Wensum Clothing, which provided the players' Wembley suits, and Rombah Wallace, which supplied the shoes to go with them.[29]

The Sunderland team were younger than Norwich's, and manager Len Ashurst was also much less experienced than Ken Brown. Nevertheless, the north-east side had had an excellent run to the final, beating Crystal Palace, Nottingham Forest, Tottenham and Watford before facing Chelsea in the semi-final. This turned out to be a dramatic tie, with Sunderland winning 2–0 at home but needing a 3–2 win at Stamford Bridge in the second leg to make it through to the final. The stars of their cup run had been Chris Turner in goal and Clive Walker, who had scored critical goals at Tottenham and Watford, and a brace at Chelsea in the semi-final.

On the day at Wembley, a fairly uneventful first half which left the score at 0–0 burst into life at the beginning of the second. An optimistic punt forward by Steve Bruce found John Deehan robbing a dithering

27 Ken Brown, 'Absolutely positive', in Mick Dennis, *Tales from the City, Volume Three* (Tales From, 2017), pp. 76, 77.

28 Ibid., p. 77.

29 Peter Mendham with Edward Couzens-Lake, *In His Own Words: Life on the Inside* (Pitch Publishing, 2019).

Player card (Figurine Panini, Football 85)
Author's collection

David Corner on the goal-line. The resulting cross fell to the feet of Asa Hartford, whose attempted shot deflected off Sunderland's Chisholm and ended up in the back of the net in front of the Norwich supporters. Cue much jumping off the sofa at home and punching the air.

A blatant handball by Dennis Van Wijk in trying to stop Sunderland skipper Barry Venison progressing in the penalty area gave Sunderland the chance to respond with a spot kick. Given Clive Walker's record, of course, we feared the worst. But from a long run-up, Walker missed, with Woods possibly getting a hand to the ball to push it on to the post. Norwich had won the Milk Cup and a place in Europe.

The photo of 34-year-old Asa Hartford drinking from a bottle of milk certainly seems to capture a moment of innocence in terms of what happened next both in that season and in the remaining years of the decade. Both sets of fans also played their part in that the friendship and camaraderie between the respective supporters made a distinct change to the ongoing incidents of crowd trouble both at home and abroad in 1985.[30]

A Slum Sport

The last few months of the 1984/85 season saw some of the most terrible events in the history of English football. On 13 March 1985 there were televised violent disturbances between fans and police at an FA Cup tie between Luton Town and Millwall. It led directly to a four-season ban on away supporters by Luton Town and to Luton's expulsion from the League Cup in 1986/87. Luton introduced a membership card scheme which Margaret Thatcher planned to force clubs to adopt nationally.

On 11 May 1985, on the final day of Bradford City's season, a fire in a wooden stand at their Valley Parade ground led to 56 fatalities and 265 others being injured. The stand had been officially condemned and had been due to be replaced. The fire started when a cigarette fell between the seats, setting fire to the litter beneath. The fire spread very quickly, with many fans trapped by locked exit gates at the back of the stand and by similarly locked turnstile gates.

30 See the report of the game in Rob Carless, *Under the Floodlights! The Story of the English Football League Cup 1960–2024* (Pitch Publishing, 2024), pp. 130–5.

Just eighteen days later, on 29 May, there was another crowd disaster at the Heysel Stadium in Brussels in which 39 fans died in a crush. The tragedy was mainly caused by the behaviour of the fans of Liverpool and Juventus at the European Cup Final. The deaths occurred when Liverpool fans charged the Italian fans, who died when a wall in the stadium collapsed, and 14 Liverpool fans were eventually convicted of assault and manslaughter. However, a report at the time noted the 'appalling state of the stadium' and three Belgians stood trial, including the head of the Belgian Football Association and two Belgian police chiefs. The secretary-general of Belgian football received a six-month suspended prison sentence for allowing tickets for the 'neutral zone' in the stadium to be sold to opposing fans whilst a gendarme captain who was in charge of policing the stands was also found guilty.

Some academics such as Ian Taylor argued at the time that 'a way of thinking, writing, and talking about the condition of British football has emerged in which the events of Bradford and Brussels are conflated'.[31] Taylor wrote that the rhetoric of Margaret Thatcher had connected hooliganism with the unregulated and badly organised condition of British working-class sport and that these events were watersheds in what he said was a fundamental disenchantment with football. The *Sunday Times*, owned by Rupert Murdoch, adopted this framing with an infamous editorial on 19 May, just eight days after the Bradford fire, which used the headline, 'Putting the boot in' and called football a 'slum sport played in slum stadiums and increasingly watched by slum people!'[32]

The Popplewell Inquiry was announced by the then Home Secretary, Leon Brittan, on 13 May 1985.[33] This was just two days after the Bradford fire and crowd trouble on the same day at Birmingham City's ground (Birmingham were playing Leeds United) in which a 15-year-old-fan, Ian Hambridge, died after a wall collapsed. A High Court judge, Mr Justice Popplewell, was appointed to lead the inquiry, which began on 5 June. It was concluded after just five and a half days. The inquests into the fatalities at Valley Parade returned a verdict of death by misadventure and no criminal prosecutions were considered. As with Hillsborough four years later, it has taken independent research and scrutiny to understand better what happened at Bradford. Martin Fletcher, who was at the match

31 Ian Taylor, 'Putting the boot into a working-class sport: British soccer after Bradford and Brussels', *Sociology of Sport Journal*, 4 (1987), p. 172.

32 *Sunday Times*, 19 May 1985.

33 Oliver Popplewell, *Committee of Inquiry into Crowd Safety and Control at Sports Grounds* (HMSO, 1986).

and lost relatives, has told a harrowing story of institutional neglect and the government's general indifference to safety at grounds at the time.[34]

Jon Spurling wrote about the Popplewell Inquiry forty years later.[35] Whilst Popplewell's report focused on regulation around fire safety, it also recommended that grounds introduce CCTV in order to monitor fan behaviour. Popplewell also recommended that football clubs introduce membership schemes which would help them gather information on fans to help their commercial activities.

Out of Europe

Norwich City's success in winning the Milk Cup at Wembley in March should have guaranteed them a place in the UEFA Cup for the first time in the following season. However, events at the end of the 1984/85 season completely changed Norwich's fortunes. Perhaps the fire which destroyed part of the Main Stand at Carrow Road in October 1984 and left it closed for the remainder of the season was an indicator of the misfortune that was to follow. The club went on a terrible run of games in which they won only two of their remaining twelve. That should still have been enough to stay in Division One, but Coventry City, who played their last three games after Norwich's season had been completed, contrived to win all of them, sending Norwich down into Division Two. It was clearly unfair that Coventry's games were played later than Norwich's, and this indeed led to a rule change. From that season on, the Football League ruled that every club would play their last match at the same time on the same date.

Finally, as a direct result of the events at Heysel, English football clubs, including Norwich, were banned from European competition from 1985 through to 1990. Norwich consulted the Professional Footballers' Association to see if they had any grounds for appeal,[36] but under a government that had no time for football, this was not an option.

34 Martin Fletcher, *Fifty-Six: The Story of the Bradford Fire* (Bloomsbury, 2015).

35 Spurling, *Go To War.*

36 Brendan Batson, *The Third Degree: My Autobiography* (Curtis Sport, 2023).

Match Report: Saturday 15 April 1989, k/o 15:00.
The FA Challenge Cup semi-final, Villa Park, Everton 1 Norwich City 0.
Attendance: 46,533.

Norwich City
Bryan Gunn, Ian Culverhouse, Mark Bowen, Ian Butterworth, Andy Linighan, Andy Townsend, Dale Gordon, Malcolm Allen (Ruel Fox), Robert Rosario, Ian Crook, Trevor Putney. Manager: Dave Stringer.

Everton
Neville Southall, Neil McDonald, Pat Van Den Hauwe, Kevin Ratcliffe, Dave Watson, Paul Bracewell, Pat Nevin, Trevor Steven, Graeme Sharp, Tony Cottee, Kevin Sheedy. Manager: Colin Harvey.

Goals
Everton: Nevin (26)

Player card
(Panini, Football 88)
Author's collection

Norwich City's time in Division Two following their relegation from the top division in 1985 was brief. With players such as Dave Watson, Chris Woods, Steve Bruce and Mark Barham remaining with the club, Ken Brown had a strong squad at his disposal. He could even afford to strengthen the squad with the signings of Mike Phelan, Kevin Drinkell and Ian Culverhouse. City finished champions of the Second Division, seven points above Charlton Athletic. Drinkell managed an impressive 22 goals from 41 league appearances. And Brown's team continued their success in the following season in Division One, finishing fifth.

During this period, Sir Arthur South had been replaced as chairman of Norwich City by Robert Chase following a series of resignations from the board over concerns about the tendering process for the reconstruction of the Main Stand. Roger Munby, a marketing director with Reckitt and Colman Ltd, was a new member.[37] *In preparation for the 1986/87 season, City announced a three-year-sponsorship deal with the Norwich Brewery Company worth £200,000 a year, during which 'Foster's Lager' would appear on the front of the players' shirts.*[38] *The league itself was now rebranded as the Today League, Division One. The new City stand opened for the first time for the Canaries' match against Southampton on 30 August 1986. There was also a family enclosure between the River End and South Stand with 378 seats and standing room for 400 – opened in time for the Canaries' match against Southampton on 30 August 1986. Bryan Gunn began*

37 Woodrow, *Norwich City Football Club*, vol. III, 3 January 1986.

38 Ibid., vol. III, 22 July 1986.

his long association with Norwich City when he was signed from Aberdeen for £100,000 in October 1986.

Despite the club's less successful start to the 1987/88 season (the league had again been renamed with a new contract with Barclays Bank), it was still perhaps a surprise that Brown was sacked after the first three months in November 1987 – City were at that time occupying a relegation spot in 19th place. Dave Stringer, a former player and then assistant team manager, was the club's slightly unexpected choice as new manager. Mike Walker, a former manager of Colchester United, became reserve team manager. Stringer ensured that Norwich remained in Division One, with the club record signing of Robert Fleck for £580,000 in December 1987 from Glasgow Rangers being a key factor, although Steve Bruce left for Manchester United for a fee of around £950,000 the same month. The club went from strength to strength in 1988/89. City's 2–1 victory against West Ham United on 27 December 1988 was their first league match to be shown live on television (on ITV).[39] Fans like myself might also remember the next time Norwich were shown live on television when they won 3–2 at Millwall in January 1989 through Robert Fleck's winner deep into injury time (I still have the video recording). In total, three of Norwich's league matches were shown live on television that season, resulting in an income of £438,750 (only four clubs received more).[40] Norwich's finishing league position of fourth that season would have qualified them for Europe had it not been for the ban. Their outstanding form also led them to their first FA Cup semi-final for thirty years.

Player card (Panini, Football 90)
Author's collection

Norwich were playing an Everton team who had had considerable experience of the big time. The 1980s was a very successful decade for the blue team on Merseyside. They had won two League titles (1984/85 and 1986/87), the European Cup Winners' Cup (1985) and the FA Cup (1984). But, like Norwich themselves, the ban on English clubs competing in European football had hit them hard. After the 1987 Division One title, Everton's manager Howard Kendall had departed to be replaced by his deputy, Colin Harvey. The team was still stacked with talent, with stalwarts such as Neville Southall, Kevin Ratcliffe, Kevin Sheedy and Trevor Steven. They were joined by old Norwich

39 Ibid., vol. III, 27 December 1988.

40 Ibid., vol. III, 1 May 1989.

favourite Dave Watson, who had moved back to Merseyside in 1986, and 1988/89 season signings Tony Cottee and Pat Nevin.

I had moved to Merseyside in 1984 and, given that it was much easier to buy tickets then, I remember queuing at Goodison Park in a mass of blue and white scarves to get a ticket for the semi-final. Whilst I would obviously have preferred to be with Norwich fans, getting into the game was my first priority. I bought three tickets for myself and two old friends from the Midlands who planned to go with me as 'neutrals'. On that April day I met Bob and Mike in central Birmingham and had a couple of pints in a city centre pub before grabbing a bus to the match. I remember that time was a bit tight and we had to rush. The Norwich supporters were in the Holte End, the home end, whilst we had tickets with the Everton fans in the North Stand. Villa Park is a magnificent old stadium built by the redoubtable Scottish stadium architect, Archibald Leitch. But, like many other stadiums of its era, some of the entry points are narrow and fans are used to several pinch points as you find your way in and out; access to the refreshment areas is particularly tight. Mike remembers being jostled by police horses on our way into the ground. We arrived a few minutes before kick-off and were shepherded down beside the supporters' pen, walked behind the goal, and were directed on to the terrace.

It was a sunny day, and I was very excited. Norwich hadn't reached an FA Cup semi-final since their famous run of 1959 when they were members of the Third Division South. Players such as Bryan Gunn, Ian Crook, Dale Gordon, Robert Fleck, Andy Townsend and Mike Phelan had been having a great season and, in early April, Norwich were even in with a chance of a league and cup double. Norwich had won 2–1 at Old Trafford in October 1988 with Andy Townsend's first goal for the club, and had followed this up at Anfield in December when another goal from Townsend marked a famous 1–0 victory. Norwich were eight places above Everton in the table. They had beaten West Ham 3–1 in a quarter-final replay to earn their shot at glory. The match programme contrasted the 'Glasgow Boys' – Graeme Sharp and Robert Fleck – who were due to play on the opposing teams. In the same programme, the Norwich manager, Dave Stringer, wrote that this would be 'a great day out for the fans'. Even the late news that Fleck wouldn't be playing – he had received the news that his father had prematurely passed away aged only 44 – didn't entirely dampen the spirit of the Norwich fans. We had very high hopes of reaching Wembley as the match kicked off to a roar from both sets of spectators at three o'clock.

The cover of the match programme for the FA Challenge Cup semi-final, Villa Park, Norwich City vs Everton, 15 April 1989

Author's collection

From that point on, my memories of the game are a series of blurred fragments, as the news from Sheffield started to reach us. Right at the beginning we were keen to hear what was happening at the other semi-final. This was a time before mobile phones when it wasn't so easy to keep track of other events. Many supporters took small battery-operated radios to matches which they held to their ears whilst trying to get a decent signal. Other people often gathered around to ask about the scores at other matches. And this was exactly the case on that day. The Evertonians in particular were keen to hear how their city rivals Liverpool were progressing in their match against Nottingham Forest, which had kicked off at the same time. So it was that the news started to spread that 'fans had started to spill on to the pitch' at Hillsborough, and then that the match had been abandoned. The first response was that this was due to trouble on the terraces. It took time to hear there had been a casualty or even a fatality. But given that many people from Merseyside, myself included, knew people at the other semi-final, the mood changed very quickly to one of concern and growing distress. When Pat Nevin scuffed a toe poke over the line for Everton after 26 minutes, I have no idea how much I knew about what was happening in Sheffield, but the match I was watching was becoming increasingly irrelevant as people were desperately trying to find out exactly what was taking place at another event altogether.

After the match, I walked around the streets by Villa Park, disorientated and upset. I remember I had a drink with Bob and Mike but not much else. I bumped into an old friend from Norwich, but we found it difficult to say anything which didn't seem empty and trivial. I wanted to get home to Liverpool as soon as I could. On the Monday I rang a Liverpool-supporting mate, Dave, to check he was OK. It turned out he hadn't gone to Hillsborough but his brother had. His brother was fine but had lost a shoe in the terrible events and crush at the Leppings Lane End.

I had heard that Liverpool supporters were going to Anfield as the city reeled in shock and disbelief. I asked Dave if he thought it would be appropriate for a Norwich fan to go in solidarity. I was very upset and wanted to be with other football fans. So it was that that week I queued for over three hours to enter Anfield to pay my respects to all those who had lost their lives because they wanted to follow their team to an FA Cup semi-final. I remember coming into the ground to be met by a carpet of flowers covering the pitch. It was profound and moving. A service was held in the stadium where everyone present sang 'You'll Never Walk Alone', a song that even now makes my eyes prick and sends a shudder down my back.

The Hillsborough Disaster

The final death toll of those caught in the terrible crush of Liverpool supporters was 97, but so many more were directly or indirectly affected. An inquest held in 1990 said that there was insufficient evidence to bring criminal charges, and the coroner's report of 1991 ruled that all the deaths had been accidental. After an independent panel was formed to review the tragedy in 2009, it was announced in 2012 that the police had covered up evidence and falsified reports in order to blame the Liverpool fans for the crush. A further inquest found in 2016 that the original 96 victims had been 'unlawfully killed' and, in 2017, criminal charges were filed against six individuals, including South Yorkshire Police Chief Superintendent David Duckenfield. Despite the behaviour and actions of the police both in 1989 and in subsequent years in denying their culpability, only one person has been convicted for actions that led to the deaths of so many fans who had simply chosen to follow their team to a football match that sunny April day. Almost thirty years after the worst stadium disaster in British history, Graham Mackrell, the Hillsborough Stadium safety officer and secretary of Sheffield Wednesday Football Club, was found guilty in 2019 of failing to take 'reasonable care' of Liverpool fans by not providing an adequate number of turnstiles. Mackrell was fined £6,500 plus £5,000 court prosecution costs.

There had been previous disasters in British football. The Ibrox disaster in Glasgow in 1971 saw 66 deaths following a crush at a Rangers vs Celtic game. A crush had occurred previously at Leppings Lane at the 1981 FA Cup semi-final between Tottenham Hotspur and Wolverhampton Wanderers in which 38 fans had suffered injuries including broken arms and legs. There had also been crowd problems at Hillsborough in subsequent semi-finals in 1987 and even in 1988 when Liverpool and Forest had also met. The ground's safety certificate had not been renewed since 1981, and the stadium's match capacity had not been changed. If there was a common factor in these disasters, it was the dilapidated state of the grounds in question and the low consideration given to fans' safety. At Bradford City exit doors were locked, whilst at Hillsborough, cages penned fans in, leading directly to the crush and their inability to escape.

Roger Domeneghetti has placed the Hillsborough disaster in the context of other disasters in the 1980s.[41] He draws attention to six other disasters between the Bradford fire and Hillsborough – such as the fire on a British Airways jet at Manchester Airport in August 1985 (55 fatalities) and a similar tragedy at King's Cross Underground station in November 1987 (31 fatalities) – and asked whether they reflected a contemporary disregard for safety and the dilapidated state of the nation's infrastructure. The poor state of football grounds and attitudes to policing certainly seemed to reflect the values of society in general. And there is a clear contradiction between a government committed to deregulation and the state's commitment to protect public safety.

Margaret Thatcher's government took a robust position on 'law and order' and strongly supported the police in their various confrontations with striking miners during the UK miners' strike of 1984 and 1985. The Battle of Orgreave on 18 June 1984 involved the South Yorkshire Police, with many reports of excessive violence used by the police against the pickets. The media coverage of the confrontation by the BBC was heavily edited to imply that the striking miners were principally responsible for the violence and was criticised both at the time and much later. It followed

41 Domeneghetti, *Everybody Wants to Rule the World.*

FOSTER'S
LAGER
hummel

Replica Hummel shirt, sponsored by Foster's Lager

Author's collection

Thatcher's argument that the miners needed to be defeated at any cost and characterised them as the 'enemy within'.[42]

In April 1989 it was the same South Yorkshire Police that were responsible for the policing of the FA Cup semi-final. And it was the coverage of the disaster by another Murdoch-owned newspaper, *The Sun*, which is most remembered for how the event was reported afterwards. Thatcher's government supported the police, and the mainstream media supported the framing of Hillsborough as being caused by the Liverpool fans. The *Daily Mail* carried the police's accusation that 'vile fans fought us as we tried to help the dying' and the *Daily Express* had similar copy: 'Police accuse drunken fans'.[43] Thatcher had been clear about where she stood on football; a sport she had no interest in. She had been committed to the introduction of a compulsory National Identity Scheme for football supporters as part of her approach to addressing football hooliganism and this helped frame how her government viewed what happened on that terrible afternoon in Sheffield. A stream of subsequent inquiries and inquests have shown the truth that police officers fabricated evidence and that a series of lies created what amounted to a huge cover-up which blamed football fans for the shortcomings and inadequacies of both the police themselves and the football stadium and its officials.

The Hillsborough disaster proved a turning point in how football was viewed and how it was governed. Lord Justice Taylor's reports in 1989 and 1990 led to a review of stadium safety. The resulting changes led to the refurbishment or reconstruction of stadiums, including the introduction of all-seater facilities. Many have described these changes as being designed to alter the fan demographic to marginalise the possibility of crowd disorder, with increased ticket prices both contributing to stadium rebuilding costs and to changing football culture.

For Norwich City, and for all other English league clubs, the future was going to be strikingly different

42 Shane Ewen and Aaron Andrews, 'The media, affect and community in a decade of disasters: reporting the 1985 Bradford City stadium fire', *Contemporary British History*, 35.2 (2021), pp. 258–83.

43 Domenghetti, *Everybody Wants to Rule the World*.

U.E.F.A.
1993-94
orwich and
terborough
BUILDING SOCIETY

THE 1990s

When Football Was Cool

When Football Was Cool

1990 John Major becomes leader of the Conservative Party; Rupert Murdoch establishes BSkyB; FIFA World Cup in Italy (featuring 'Nessun Dorma' on the BBC coverage); New Order's 'World in Motion' is recorded by the England team

1992 *Fever Pitch* by Nick Hornby is published; the establishment of the English Premier League; the UEFA Champions League (formerly the European Cup) is formed

1993 'Let's Kick Racism Out of Football' campaign; Norwich City's first (and only) participation in European competition

1994 Fantasy Football League, presented by David Baddiel and Frank Skinner, on the BBC; BBC Radio 5 Live launches in March 1994

1995 Talksport (formerly Talk Radio UK) on the airwaves; Bosman ruling establishes greater freedom of movement of players

1996 'Three Lions' (David Baddiel and Frank Skinner) reaches Number 1; Euro '96 in England; Delia Smith joins the board of Norwich City

1997 Tony Blair becomes Prime Minister in May; Death of Diana, Princess of Wales in August

1998 The FA removes the restrictions on dividends and on directors working part-time from its rule book

Previous spread: Replica of Norwich City's shirt as worn in the UEFA Cup, 1993-94 and background of front cover of match programme, Norwich City vs Bayern Munich, 3rd November 1993

Author's collections

From Year Zero to Cool Britannia

In November 1990 Margaret Thatcher was deposed as leader of the Conservative Party and replaced by John Major, who went on to win the General Election in 1992. But Thatcher's legacy was all too clear: a rallying cry for personal choice and individual freedoms, deregulation, and a green flag for profits to be made by private investors across a range of previously nationally owned assets. The role of the state in supporting the country's most vulnerable communities was much eroded. The mantra was the survival of the strong at the expense of the weak.

Football's governing body, the Football Association, understood the prevailing mood as well as anyone else. *The Blueprint for the Future of Football*, which was published in June 1991, is a clear statement of how those responsible for football now saw its future.[1] The authors of *The Blueprint* argued that whilst football clubs had expressed the needs of local communities and had indeed formed a part of social provision in the past, the future needed to include safer all-seater stadiums and a radical transformation of football to develop its commercial potential.

In contrast to the terrible tragedies affecting English football in the previous decade, the television coverage of the FIFA Men's World Cup, held in Italy in the summer of 1990, showed the entertainment spectacle that a well-packaged football tournament could provide. Despite the overall poor quality of the football, Italia '90 achieved record television figures, thanks in part to the BBC's use of Luciano Pavarotti singing 'Nessun Dorma'. The England team recorded 'World in Motion' with New Order, featuring John Barnes rapping; arguably the only time an English football team recorded anything fashionable. The team, under Bobby Robson, also performed well on the pitch by reaching the semi-finals, eventually crashing out to West Germany in a penalty shootout which is as much remembered for Paul Gascoigne's tears as the team's loss. Nick Hornby's book *Fever Pitch* in 1992 found the middle classes beginning to chatter excitedly about football. At the same time football fanzines were taking football writing to new audiences by directly involving fans. Television and radio were also catching up with the sport's prospective new audiences. 'Fantasy Football League' on television, BBC Radio 5 Live and Talk Radio all found their place, reflecting the growing appetite for the latest news and information as well as football banter. The sport was entering the national consciousness, but in a good way this time.

1 The Football Association, *The Blueprint for the Future of Football* (The Football Association, 1991).

The establishment of the English Premier League for the 1992/93 football season has been written about by many of those involved, including the then chief executive of the Professional Footballers' Association, Gordon Taylor, who saw the new league as 'a way for the leading clubs to seize virtually all the money'.[2] The decision by the FA in September 1991 to allow the top 22 clubs to break away to form a new elite league undoubtedly revolutionised football, but for others it highlighted the development of 'questionable and predatory business methods' to fully exploit and commodify all aspects of the game.[3] In effect, it was a breakaway league, as were the proposed European Super League plans of the future. The FA, in attempting to assert its authority over the Football League, had scored a massive own goal in enabling the new league to be formed. Within a year the FA had no say in the Premier League's operation and there were three completely separate power centres in English football – the new Premier League, the FA and the rump of the Football League.[4] Much of this history has been either forgotten or rewritten though. And for many younger writers and fans, this was when the history of modern English football began: its own 'Year Zero'.

American sport had shown the way in the 1980s, and television was about to get into bed with football in a big way. Rupert Murdoch's winning bid to acquire the broadcasting rights to live coverage of the new English Premier League for BSkyB in 1992 was literally a game-changer. Murdoch's News Corporation had already used 'sports as a "battering ram" and a lead offer in all [its] pay television operations' to develop an audience for satellite television.[5] It wasn't until the pandemic interrupted the Premier League season of 2019/20 that live football league action again appeared on our free-to-view television screens. But back in the 1990s, BSkyB's (Sky) portrayal of football was like a dramatic new entertainment product exploding on to our screens. However, the launch of 'Kick It Out' in 1993 showed that football had not completely managed to shake off the racist and less savoury elements of its recent past.

Tony Blair's landslide election victory of May 1997 changed nothing about the governance of sport or indeed the Thatcherite push towards free markets, but Blair's government did help to promote football as part of

2 Quoted in David Conn, *The Beautiful Game? Searching for the Soul of Football* (Yellow Jersey Press, 2005), p. 102.

3 Tom Bower, *Broken Dreams: Vanity, Greed and the Souring of British Football* (Simon & Schuster, 2003).

4 See Alex Fynn and Lynton Guest, *Out of Time: Why Football isn't Working* (Simon & Schuster, 1994), for a detailed description of the football authorities' machinations at this time.

5 David. L. Andrews, 'Sport and the transnationalizing media corporation', *The Journal of Media Economics*, 16.4 (2003), p. 239.

the 'Cool Britannia' rebranding of popular culture. Diana, Princess of Wales, had captured the popular imagination – in Blair's phrase, she was 'the people's princess' – and was part of the cultural and political sea change that helped bring Labour to power. Diana's death in August 1997 seems symbolic – in retrospect – of a loss of faith in big institutions and government as conspiracy theories proliferated. Princess Diana and popular culture were perhaps at their zenith, and so the nation wept whilst neoliberalism was on the march in both football and the economic practices of Western governments.

A Whole New Ball Game

The new satellite coverage of what was originally known as the FA Premier League launched in a fizz of multi-coloured shirts and new camera angles. Dancing girls, borrowed from American sport, arrived on pitches at half-time, pundits in TV studios were loud and forthright. And, of course, first the English public, and then a much wider global audience, were encouraged to buy satellite dishes to watch the action.

BSkyB's new coverage included a 'Super Sunday' with matches kicking off one after other in the afternoon. The first game shown was Nottingham Forest vs Liverpool on 16 August 1992, using a new digital onscreen graphic showing the score and the time elapsed in the match. On the following day, the satellite station launched its Monday Night Football programme allowing it to broadcast a live match from the Premier League (the first was Manchester City vs Queens Park Rangers). Both shows were direct copies of weekly broadcasts of the National Football League in the United States and were funded by sponsorship and advertising. The bigger clubs had been advocating for a larger slice of the income from football and the Premier League gave them this on a very large new plate. The fees received from TV rights would be the bedrock of Premier League clubs' income for years to come, and they could base their commercial revenue on guaranteeing their shirt sponsors brand publicity on television screens. But some clubs, such as Manchester United and Liverpool – which were becoming commercial brands themselves – were on television much more than others. The financial gap between the Premier League members and the Football League was beginning to grow, as was that between the big city clubs and the smaller, provincial, less fashionable teams in England's elite professional competition.

The Norwich City fanzine 'Liverpool Are On The Tele Again' played on the fact that bigger clubs received much more television coverage and thus more income

This edition is from 1996

Author's collection

Standing, Seating and Sales

In hindsight, the Hillsborough disaster in 1989 seemed an almost inevitable end to a terrible sequence of accidents and injuries which had occurred previously on British sports grounds. Simon Inglis noted at least 282 fatalities and 4,000 injuries from 35 incidents at 29 different grounds before Hillsborough (including another crush at the same ground resulting in 75 fans needing hospital treatment as far back as 1914).[6] A Safety of Sports Grounds Act was passed in 1975, but it appeared to have had little impact. Lord Justice Taylor's subsequent reports on stadium safety led directly to the refurbishment and reconstruction of all the Premier League stadiums, including Carrow Road.[7]

Norwich City's first professional home was the first enclosed sports ground in Norfolk at Newmarket Road, where they played their matches from 1905 to 1908, after which they moved into a new ground called The Nest, in a space formerly occupied by a disused chalk pit. Even then there were significant safety issues (there was a serious accident involving about 60 fans in 1922), and the club were forced to move in 1935 when part of the pitch collapsed because of the old chalk workings.[8] A new purpose-built stadium at Carrow Road was opened in 1935 on land owned by Colman's Mustard, although it was then sub-let to the Boulton Paul engineering company. In 1971 Norwich City purchased the freehold of the land and, just one year later, they were promoted to Division One for

Carrow Road in 1962 with the old River End open terrace. Image taken from cover of Norwich City vs Middlesbrough match programme, 29th December 1962

Author's collection

6 Simon Inglis, *Football Grounds of Britain, Third Edition* (CollinsWillow, 1996), p. 9.

7 Lord Justice Peter Taylor, *Inquiry into the Hillsborough Stadium Disaster: Final Report* (HMSO, 1990).

8 Inglis, *Football Grounds of Britain*, p. 269.

the first time. Ground improvements included the new River End Stand, complete with executive boxes and offices, which replaced the River End open terrace in 1979. The City Stand (subsequently renamed the Geoffrey Watling Stand in honour of the former Norwich City president) was built to replace the Main Stand which had been destroyed by fire in 1984, and a new Barclay Stand (named after a former club vice-president, Captain Evelyn Barclay) was opened in 1993. The latter was built with the assistance of a grant of £2 million from the Football Trust and was developed to satisfy the government ruling that stadiums now needed to be all-seater to fulfil the safety requirements proposed in the Taylor Report. This was arguably the principal legacy of Robert Chase during his time as chairman. Whilst players were sold, money was found to spend on land acquisition around Carrow Road and stadium and training ground improvements. The Football Trust grant also funded the installation of CCTV cameras.

Whilst safety was rightly seen to be at the heart of developments at Carrow Road, ground developments, such as the new stand in 1979, usually included more opportunities to maximise revenue from additional facilities such as new executive boxes. As stadium facilities, including provision for the new media requirements, were improved across the Premier League, the emphasis was on meeting corporate needs. The monetising schemes included catering to a more affluent clientele. Whilst football grounds were critical to clubs' heritage and identities, stadiums were being gradually transformed to welcome fans, but as customers and consumers. John Bale from Keele University wrote in 1991 that the introduction of seating was a move towards containment and discipline, and that the modern sport stadium would be safe and comfortable but somehow also inauthentic.[9] Certainly, many supporters felt that seated stadiums affected the match atmosphere and this led to dissatisfaction from the most vociferous fans. Gestures and words were also now policed.[10] Football's new laws included the offence of making 'racial or indecent chants' at a match, a move which was well-meaning in theory but incredibly difficult to put into practice.[11]

There were many more opportunities for advertising in the Premier League stadiums. Manchester United had first installed billboards around Old

9 John Bale, 'Playing at home: British football and a sense of place', in John Williams and Stephen Wagg (eds), *British Football and Social Change: Getting into Europe* (Leicester University Press, 1991).

10 Clive Norris, Jade Moran and Gary Armstrong, *Surveillance, Closed Circuit Television and Social Control* (Routledge, 2020).

11 The 'new laws' were set out in Norwich City's matchday programme for Norwich City vs Chelsea, 19 August 1992 (the opening game of the season at Carrow Road).

Liverpool's famous Spion Kop stand was converted into an all-seater stand in 1994. The Kop had been opened complete with roof on 25 August, 1928. The final match with the standing Kop was against Norwich City on 30th April, 1994. Norwich won 1-0 with a trademark volley from Jeremy Goss (as witnessed by the author).

Author's collection

Trafford in 1975, in a contract with Admiral.[12] By the end of the 1990s the new and refurbished grounds were installing LED digital displays to amplify and enhance the brands of clubs' commercial sponsors, reaching out to matchgoers and television viewers alike.

The Norwich & Peterborough Building Society began their five-year shirt sponsorship with Norwich City in 1992. It replaced the three-year deal with the Japanese sports clothing firm Asics from the 1989/90 season. The deal included their logo on the front of the players' shirts, and club match tickets to be sold through 26 of the building society's branch offices.[13] In 1997 the River End Stand became the Norwich & Peterborough Stand, the first section of the Carrow Road stadium to be sponsored. Fans who opened a savings account (a 'Canary Account') with the building society saw a percentage of any interest earned donated to the club.[14]

Match Report: Monday 5 April 1993, k/o 19:45.
The FA Premier League, Carrow Road, Norwich City 1 Manchester United 3.
Attendance: 20,582.

Norwich City
Bryan Gunn, Ian Culverhouse, Mark Bowen, John Polston, Gary Megson (Efan Ekoku), Ian Crook, David Phillips, Jeremy Goss, Mark Robins, Ruel Fox, Chris Sutton. Manager: Mike Walker.

Manchester United
Peter Schmeichel, Denis Irwin, Paul Parker, Steve Bruce, Gary Pallister, Paul Ince, Lee Sharpe, Andrei Kanchelskis (Bryan Robson), Ryan Giggs, Brian McClair, Eric Cantona. Manager: Alex Ferguson.

Goals
Norwich City: Robins (61)
Manchester United: Giggs (13), Kanchelskis (20), Cantona (21)

Norwich City were one of the founder members of the Premier League. Dave Stringer had kept the club in the top league since his appointment in 1987; Norwich had enjoyed their longest period in Division One

12 Claude Boli, 'Manchester United: the capitalized history, from the 1960s to today', in Nicolas Chanavat, Michel Desbordes and Nicolas Lorgnier (eds), *Routledge Handbook of Football Marketing* (Routledge, 2017).

13 James Woodrow (as compiled for the Norwich City Football Club), *Norwich City Football Club: The Archive* (Severn, 2022), vol. III, 24 June 1992.

14 Ibid., vol. III, 12 March 1997.

since the 1970s. Robert Chase, who had taken over as chair of the club from Sir Arthur South in 1985, had already shown himself to be very astute in his dealings, as the Tottenham Hotspur chairman of this time – Irving Scholar – ruefully reflected.[15] *However, Norwich had finished the 1991/92 season in 18th place only three points clear of Luton Town, one of three clubs relegated (the others were Notts County and West Ham United). Norwich had reached the FA Cup semi-final in April 1992, but lost out to Second Division Sunderland. That must have hurt, and no doubt was one of the reasons why Stringer resigned at the end of the season, but there was also the loss of players such as Steve Bruce, Mike Phelan, Andy Townsend and Dale Gordon, all sold to balance Chase's books. As Stringer himself says, he left out of 'total frustration'.*[16] *The appointment of Mike Walker as the new manager – promoted from being the club's reserve team manager – was a surprise. The position was going to be offered to Phil Neal, the former Liverpool player, but he was not prepared to relocate from his home on Merseyside.*[17]

When club favourite Robert Fleck went to Chelsea for £2.1 million before the season began, it is fair to say that there were not high expectations for the Canaries and, indeed, they were one of the pre-season favourites for relegation.

I was working away during the first match of the season when Norwich played Arsenal. The Canaries were 0–2 down at half-time and absolutely no one expected what happened next. By the time I had a chance to check the score again on television we had won 4–2, with new signing Mark Robins coming on to score two goals, including an outrageous chip over David Seaman. Remarkably, City went on to win seven of their opening games in that first Premier League season, including recording an early double against Chelsea.

The Canaries were top in September and, after 18 games, were eight points clear. That lead would have secured them the title in most other Premier League seasons – the only greater swings have been in 2018/19, when Manchester City pulled back a 9-point gap on Liverpool; in 1997/98, when Arsenal chased down 11 points to catch Manchester United; and in 1995/96 when Kevin Keegan's Newcastle United blew a remarkable 12-point lead over Alex Ferguson's United.

15 Irving Scholar with Mihir Bose, *Behind Closed Doors* (André Deutsch, 1992).

16 Rick Waghorn, *12 Canary Greats: Reflections from their Glory Days* (Jarrold Publishing and Norwich City Football Club, 2004), p. 65.

17 Woodrow, *Norwich City Football Club*, vol. III, 1 June 1992.

The front cover of the match programme for Norwich City vs Manchester United, 5th April 1993

Author's collection

When the Premier League was formed, there were still opportunities for clubs such as Wimbledon and Oldham Athletic. The oldest professional football club in the world, Notts County, had only been relegated from Division One the previous season; the beginning of their journey to non-league football, where they stayed for four years until 2023. Wimbledon no longer exist as established in 1992 (their relocation to Milton Keynes in 2004 led to the formation of a new AFC

Wimbledon), and Oldham fell as far as The National League, the fifth level of the English football league system.

Norwich had what can only be described as an inconsistent autumn in that first Premier League season. They played Blackburn Rovers at Ewood Park in front of 16,312 spectators – including myself – in early October, when Alan Shearer, in his pomp, ripped through the Norwich defence, with the Lancashire club recording a 7–1 win. Another 4–1 loss at Liverpool the same month seriously damaged Norwich's goal difference.

The first game I attended that was broadcast live on Sky television was Oldham vs Norwich at Boundary Park on a cold November evening in that 1992/93 season. The match featured fireworks immediately before the kick-off and half-time entertainment of actors charging each other wearing giant inflatable Sumo warrior suits. It was clear then that the future of the Premier League was probably not going to be too rosy if it regularly featured Oldham playing Norwich in front of a crowd of just 11,018. Mark Robins, a native of nearby Ashton-under-Lyne, made sure the Canaries went back to the top of the league with a superb hat-trick. His final last-minute long-range chip secured a 3–2 win, with the away fans ecstatic.

Even allowing for a poor run over Christmas, City were still vying for the title with Aston Villa and Manchester United in the spring. An edgy 1–0 win over Villa in late March – an unlikely winner coming from centre back John Polston – left Norwich top of the table on my birthday on 31 March, with a potential title decider with Manchester United coming up on 5 April.

The teams that started that match included Bryan Gunn in goal for Norwich, a young Chris Sutton, Jeremy Goss, Ruel Fox, and top goal-scorer Mark Robins, bought from Manchester United to replace Robert Fleck. The United team might be better remembered in Premier League folklore. It included Peter Schmeichel, Steve Bruce, Paul Ince, Andrei Kanchelskis, Ryan Giggs and Eric Cantona; the latter had signed from Leeds United in November 1992 and was pivotal to United's eventual first league title since 1967.

For those of us who were at Carrow Road that April evening for a match covered by Sky, the excitement was off the scale. There were only six matches remaining after the Man Utd game and a win would have put us five points clear of them (although they would have had a game in hand). But, in a staggering first 20 minutes, the home defence was destroyed by a Manchester United attack that totally bypassed Norwich's midfield, with goals in a stupendous seven-minute spell from Giggs, Kanchelskis and Cantona. A sole second-half response by Mark Robins was not enough. As Jeremy Goss wrote later in his autobiography, 'They (United) tore us apart. It was, by far, one of the best performances of any team I've ever played against in my career.'[18]

Norwich's dream was over, whilst the modern Alex Ferguson legend was just beginning. Norwich went on to finish third (after Manchester United and Aston Villa), their highest ever finish in the top league, and finally qualified for Europe after being denied three times before by the ban on English clubs in the 1980s.

Reflecting on that first ever final Premier League table in 1992/93, you appreciate that competition was so much tighter then and, of course, that more 'smaller' clubs featured. Norwich finished third, Queens Park Rangers were fifth, Wimbledon were mid-table in 12th and Oldham Athletic stayed up until the following season, when they were relegated with the newly promoted Swindon Town. The title winners, Manchester United, dropped 42 points from 42 matches (six defeats and 12 draws), whilst Norwich lost 12 matches overall and, although finishing third, had a negative goal difference. The bottom club in 1992/93 were Nottingham Forest who finished with 40 points, 44 points behind United's 84. Thirty years later, in 2022/23, Manchester City were top with 89 points from 38 matches (four fewer matches than in 1992/93), losing 25 points over the season. Southampton, who finished bottom, accumulated 25 points, no less than 64 points below Manchester City. The relative closeness in competition in 1992 had become a chasm by 2022. Match attendances have also changed considerably in this time. For example, when Eric Cantona made his debut for Manchester United when they played Norwich at Old Trafford on 12 December 1992, it was in front of a crowd of 34,500. The last time the two sides met in the Premier League was on 16 April 2022, when 73,381 cheered a 3–2 United victory in Manchester, with Cristiano Ronaldo scoring a hat-trick.

Player card
(Merlin Shooting Stars)
Author's collection

18 Jeremy Goss with Edward Couzens-Lake, *Gossy: The Autobiography* (Amberley, 2014), p. 111.

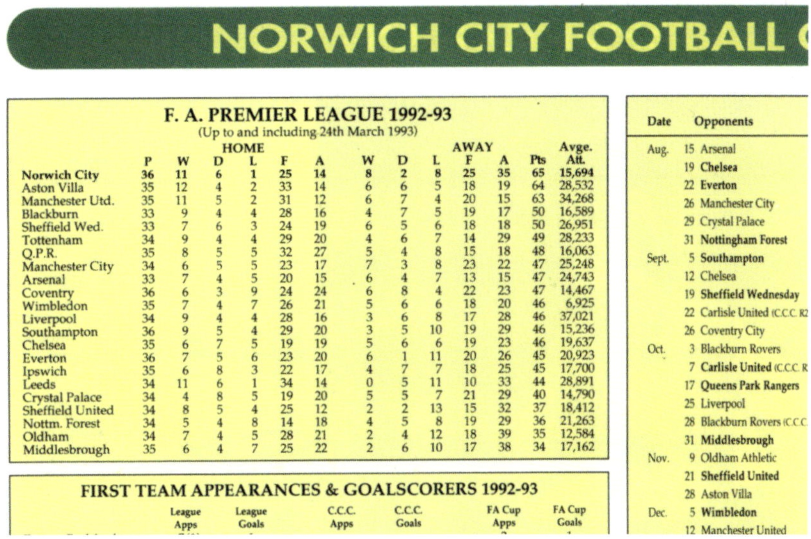

NORWICH CITY FOOTBALL

F. A. PREMIER LEAGUE 1992-93
(Up to and including 24th March 1993)

	HOME						AWAY						
	P	W	D	L	F	A	W	D	L	F	A	Pts	Avge. Att.
Norwich City	**36**	**11**	**6**	**1**	**25**	**14**	**8**	**2**	**8**	**25**	**35**	**65**	**15,694**
Aston Villa	35	12	4	2	33	14	6	6	5	18	19	64	28,532
Manchester Utd.	35	11	5	2	31	12	6	7	4	20	15	63	34,268
Blackburn	33	9	4	4	28	16	4	7	5	19	17	50	16,589
Sheffield Wed.	33	7	6	3	24	19	6	5	6	18	18	50	26,951
Tottenham	34	9	4	4	29	20	4	6	7	14	29	49	28,233
Q.P.R.	35	8	5	5	32	27	5	4	8	15	18	48	16,063
Manchester City	34	6	5	5	23	17	7	3	8	23	22	47	25,248
Arsenal	33	7	4	5	20	15	6	4	7	13	15	47	24,743
Coventry	36	6	3	9	24	24	6	8	4	22	23	47	14,467
Wimbledon	35	7	4	7	26	21	5	6	6	18	20	46	6,925
Liverpool	34	9	4	4	28	16	3	6	8	17	28	46	37,021
Southampton	36	9	5	4	29	20	3	5	10	19	29	46	15,236
Chelsea	35	6	7	5	19	19	5	6	6	19	23	46	19,637
Everton	36	7	5	6	23	20	6	1	11	20	26	45	20,923
Ipswich	35	6	8	3	22	17	4	7	7	18	25	45	17,700
Leeds	34	11	6	1	34	14	0	5	11	10	33	44	28,891
Crystal Palace	34	4	8	5	19	20	5	5	7	21	29	40	14,790
Sheffield United	34	8	5	4	25	12	2	2	13	15	32	37	18,412
Nottm. Forest	34	5	4	8	14	18	4	5	8	19	29	36	21,263
Oldham	34	7	4	5	28	21	2	4	12	18	39	35	12,584
Middlesbrough	35	6	4	7	25	22	2	6	10	17	38	34	17,162

FIRST TEAM APPEARANCES & GOALSCORERS 1992-93

	League Apps	League Goals	C.C.C. Apps	C.C.C. Goals	FA Cup Apps	FA Cup Goals

Date	Opponents
Aug.	15 Arsenal
	19 **Chelsea**
	22 **Everton**
	26 Manchester City
	29 Crystal Palace
	31 **Nottingham Forest**
Sept.	5 **Southampton**
	12 Chelsea
	19 **Sheffield Wednesday**
	22 Carlisle United (C.C.C. R2
	26 Coventry City
Oct.	3 Blackburn Rovers
	7 **Carlisle United** (C.C.C. R
	17 **Queens Park Rangers**
	25 Liverpool
	28 Blackburn Rovers (C.C.C.
	31 **Middlesbrough**
Nov.	9 Oldham Athletic
	21 **Sheffield United**
	28 Aston Villa
Dec.	5 **Wimbledon**
	12 Manchester United

The F.A. Premier League 1992/93 positions up to and including 24th March 1993, from Norwich City vs Manchester United programme, 5th April 1993

Author's collection

Under the Influence

Norwich opened the 1993/94 season with a fixture against Manchester United (going on to lose 0–2). The Premier League had sold the naming rights to their competition, so the match was in the FA Carling Premiership. Beer companies have never been slow to identify themselves with football clubs and their fans, as Tony Collins and Wray Vamplew describe in their cultural history of sport and alcohol.[19] Indeed, as far back as 1981, 32 brewers reported that they sponsored association football in some way.[20] In their highly critical account of English football published in 1994, Alex Fynn and Lynton Guest argued that the brewer's sponsorship of the Premier League in 1993, having already had a proposal rejected in 1992, was wrong in that it undermined the integrity of the competition.[21] Carling, part of the North American Molson Coors multinational which owned Bass, were the title sponsors of the Premier League from 1993 to 2001.

And, of course, companies pay good money for their sponsorship because they want a return on their investment. Bass reported just that.[22] In 1998 sales of its Carling lager had risen by 31% to become the UK's top-

19 Tony Collins and Wray Vamplew, *Mud, Sweat and Beers: A Cultural History of Sport and Alcohol* (Berg, 2002).

20 The Central Council of Physical Recreation, *Committee of Enquiry into Sports Sponsorship: "The Howell Report"* (The Central Council of Physical Recreation, 2003).

21 Fynn and Guest, *Out of Time.*

22 Collins and Vamplew, *Mud, Sweat and Beers.*

selling alcoholic brand. Carling was also the official beer of the England team during Euro '96 when sales increased by 72%. Football has never been slow to associate itself with any money that might be available, whatever the morality of associating sport with alcohol, or with the tobacco industry before that.

Why England Needed to be in Europe

The years during which English clubs were banned from Europe following the Heysel disaster were extremely damaging for English football, not least for Norwich City, who would have qualified for Europe on three occasions in this time, as League Cup winners in 1985, and then based on league position in 1986/87 (when they finished fifth) and in 1989/90 (fourth). Whilst European football was not as rewarding financially as it would be in years to come, this was still a serious blow for Norwich and many other clubs in terms of building their club brand overseas and attracting new players. UEFA lifted the ban on English clubs competing in Europe in 1990 (Liverpool were banned for an additional year) following the World Cup in Italy, where there were no significant problems presented by the English fans who attended. And by then, violence and hooliganism at matches was occurring in many other countries. UEFA wanted English football clubs back in Europe, and they certainly needed to be there.

UEFA established the first European Cup in 1956, with Real Madrid dominating its early years. The 1960 European Cup Final was played at Hampden Park in Glasgow, when Real's famous 7–3 win over Eintracht Frankfurt was attended by 127,621 spectators and was covered by the BBC. Celtic were the first British team to win the competition in 1967, with Manchester United the winners the following year. The Manchester club's victory ten years after the Munich air disaster, with two survivors – Bobby Charlton and Bill Foulkes – playing, and with Matt Busby as manager, was critical in the construction of Manchester United's history and brand. In the 1970s and the first half of the 1980s, British clubs were dominant in European competition. Liverpool won the European Cup in 1977 and 1978, followed by Nottingham Forest under Brian Clough in 1979 and 1980. Liverpool won again in 1981 and 1984, and Aston Villa were European champions in 1982.

UEFA based its qualification for the UEFA Cup (now the Europa League) on a country's previous success in the competition. Given the success of English clubs in European competition prior to the Heysel ban, England had been allocated four places. Following the ban, there were only two places available. The absence of English clubs from European competition hit hard economically as well as damaging their profile. It was another reason why bigger clubs were pushing hard for the formation of the Premier League as part of England's re-entry to European football.

The European Cup was renamed the UEFA Champions' League in 1992/93 following the sale of marketing and TV rights. The competition format now included a seeded group stage (introduced in 1991/92) to replace the first-round knockout phase. It was already being argued that this favoured the bigger clubs who would no longer be drawn against each other in the first phase of the tournament.[23] European club football continued to change throughout the 1990s[24] with more preliminary rounds in the Champions League introduced to accommodate the new nations of Eastern Europe and more teams entering directly to the group stages (16). By 1997/98, with the threat of a European Super League being formed by Europe's larger clubs, the group stage was further increased to 24 teams and league runners-up could enter the qualifying round of the Champions League. Qualification for Europe generates direct income from UEFA. For example, Banks noted that the participating clubs in the Champions League in the 1997/98 season received £100 million from UEFA.[25] Entry into European competition also increases status, providing clubs with opportunities to reach transnational audiences. For the new Premier League, reaching a global audience would prove to be critical in securing overseas television broadcasting rights.[26]

Canary Wings Across Europe

Mike Walker had hoped to bring in new players to prepare for Norwich City's first season in Europe but had not received the support he had hoped for from Robert Chase, according to Jeremy Goss's account of this time.[27] Norwich had even lost their second highest scorer from 1992/93, David Phillips (Phillips had been a £550,000 club record signing when he arrived from Coventry City in July 1989). Whilst the manager's piece in the match programme for the opening match of the new season in August 1993 (against Manchester United) focused on the players he could draw on, the chairman's message started with the improvements that had been made to the playing surface and other construction projects in the stands and car park. Chase also did not endear himself

23 See Peter Waring, *English Clubs in Europe* (independently published, 2019).

24 Anthony King, *The European Ritual: Football in the New Europe* (Routledge, 2018).

25 Simon Banks, *Going Down: Football in Crisis, How the Game Went from Boom to Bust* (Mainstream, 2002).

26 Peter Millward, *The Global Football League: Transnational Networks, Social Movements and Sport in the New Media Age* (Palgrave Macmillan, 2011).

27 Goss, *Gossy.*

to more progressive fans by announcing in the press that Norwich City would not be signing up for the new 'Let's Kick Racism Out of Football' campaign which had been launched by the Commission for Racial Equality and the Professional Footballers' Association.[28] It had taken football several years to admit that it had a problem, but clubs were finally accepting that steps needed to be put in place to address racism. Chase's argument that there was no need for such a campaign matches some of the modern dinosaurs who argued that Black Lives Matter also was unnecessary. I wonder what Ruel Fox, a brilliant talented midfielder who made 173 appearances for Norwich between 1986 and 1994, made of his chairman's comments. Fox has talked about the racist comments he received from some of his fellow youth players when he first joined the club.[29]

Robert Rosario, who played for Norwich in this same period – scoring ITV's goal of the season for his 25-yard screamer for City against Southampton on 9 September 1989 – was the first player of South Asian heritage to play in the Premier League (for Coventry City). Rosario spoke of that time to Sky News recently: 'People didn't know if I was black, white, Asian, Indian, Pakistani. There was a lot of grief, there was a lot of racism.'[30]

Norwich had squeaked into the UEFA Cup after all those years of missing out. Indeed, their qualification had only been secured at the very end of the first Premier League season. Manchester United, as inaugural Premier League champions, had already taken the Champions League place. Aston Villa had received the first UEFA Cup place available to an English club side as they had finished runners-up to United. At this time, the other place went to the winners of the League Cup, whilst the winners of the FA Cup qualified for the European Cup Winners' Cup – the latter was scrapped in 1999/2000, enabling an expanded Champions League and UEFA Cup. As Arsenal won both domestic cups – including a headed goal from former Canary defender Andy Lineghan in extra time of the FA Cup Final to secure Arsenal the double – they entered the Cup Winners' Cup, going on to win it. Arsenal's success in both the League

28 Edward Couzens-Lake, *Norwich City: The Nineties* (Amberley, 2017).

29 Ruel Fox, 'From abuse to beating Bayern', in Mick Dennis (ed.), *Tales from the City, Volume Two: A Collection of Writing about Norwich City Football Club* (Tales From, 2016).

30 Miriam Walker-Khan, '"I wanted to be white and English" – the story of Robert Rosario: the Premier League's first South Asian player', Sky Sports, 17 May 2024. Available at: https://www.skysports.com/amp/football/news/11095/13135501/i-wanted-to-be-white-and-english-the-story-of-robert-rosario-the-premier-leagues-first-south-asian-player (accessed 14 May 2025).

Cup and FA Cup left the second UEFA Cup place to Norwich. They had had to wait nearly ten years for this opportunity, but when it came, they grabbed it with both hands.

Player card
Author's collection

At the start of the 1993/94 Norwich City had enjoyed big away wins at Leeds United (4–0) and Sheffield Wednesday (5–1), and had only suffered two defeats, lying ninth in the table by the time the club's European adventure began at home to Vitesse Arnhem on 15 September. Perhaps Norwich fans were not expecting this to be Norwich's only European adventure, and Vitesse were not a big draw. There were only 16,818 at Carrow Road to witness Norwich's 3–0 win (second-half goals from Ekoku, Goss and Polston) in a match sponsored by Dutch Airline KLM and by AirUK – Norwich were keen to maximise their income from the competition wherever possible. The match programme includes a full-page advertisement for Lucozade Sport, 'Official Sports Drink of Norwich City FC'. So-called sports drinks and sugary drinks have wanted to be associated with sport since Coca-Cola's showing at the 1928 Olympics![31]

Other companies capitalising on Norwich's European success and paying for space in the Vitesse Arnhem match programme included Hummel (official boot sponsors) and Mitre (footballs). AirUK was a regional airline operating between 1980 and 1998 before being absorbed by KLM. Oh, and Coca-Cola launched a Mini-Soccer Centre at this same time, as promoted by the club's Football in the Community programme. Whilst no doubt boys and girls aged between 6 and 11 years of age did develop their footballing skills at the hourly sessions offered, the soft drinks company will have been hoping to find new young customers. Norwich City's club shop also wanted a slice of the action. You could buy a white Europe T-shirt for £12.99 (a black version cost only £7.99), a European baseball cap for £3.99, and an enamel badge for just £2.00.

Back on the pitch, after an uneventful draw in Holland in front of 9,133 spectators (Arnhem's Nieuw-Monnikenhuize stadium has long been replaced, but in 1993 it could hold a maximum of 18,000 with the addition of extra seating), the Canaries were through to the next round to face Bayern Munich. Now these were European giants. The German side had been European Cup runners-up in 1982 and 1987 and had won Bundesliga titles as recently as 1988/89 and 1989/90.

31 See the Paris Olympics website: https://olympics.com/ioc/partners/coca-cola-mengniu (accessed 14 May 2025).

Lucozade Sport. 'Official Sport Drink of Norwich City FC. Pictured from left to right, Mark Robins, Tim Sheppard (Physiotherapist) and Ian Culverhouse. Advert in match programme, Norwich City vs SBV Vitesse Arnhem, 15th September 1993, page 6

Author's collection

Front cover of match programme, Norwich City vs Bayern Munich, 3rd November 1993
Author's collection

Norwich City pin. One of the many collectables from Norwich City's experiences in the UEFA Cup in 1993/94
Author's collection

Match Report: Wednesday 3 November 1993, k/o 19:10.
UEFA Cup Second Round, Second Leg, Carrow Road, Norwich City 1 Bayern Munich 1. Attendance: 20,829.

Norwich City
Bryan Gunn, Ian Culverhouse, Mark Bowen, Ian Butterworth, John Polston, Rob Newman, Darren Eadie (Ade Akinbiyi), Ian Crook, Chris Sutton, Ruel Fox (Daryl Sutch), Jeremy Goss.
Manager: Mike Walker.

Bayern Munich
Raimond Aumann, Jorginho, Christian Ziege, Oliver Kreuzer, Thomas Helmer, Christian Nerlinger, Jan Wouters (Michael Sternkopf), Markus Schupp, Marcel Witeczek (Mehmet Scholl), Lothar Matthäus, Adolfo Valencia.
Coach: Erich Ribbeck.

Goals
Norwich City: Goss (50)
Bayern Munich: Valencia (7)

The first leg had been played at Bayern's Olympic Stadium, where the Germans had never been defeated by an English club. Bayern Munich – although not the European power they had been – still boasted a host of international players including Jorginho (Brazil), Thomas Helmer, Christian Ziege, Lothar Matthäus (all Germany), Jan Wouters (Holland) and Adolfo Valencia (Colombia). Remarkably, with goals from Jeremy Goss and Mark Bowen, the former a magnificent volley, Norwich won 2–1 in Germany. As John Motson said in a BBC commentary, 'unbelievable stuff'. As Bryan Gunn recalled, Motson went on to say that the Norwich performance was 'One of the finest displays by an English club away from home in recent years.'[32] *Neither the Norwich goalkeeper nor any Canary fans were arguing with that assessment.*

The second leg was played at Carrow Road a fortnight later and was sponsored by the city's new Audi centre, Robinsons' Audi. Being a German manufactured car, this may have provoked dual loyalties for Robinsons' staff. In the match programme, Trevor Bond, the club's marketing and promotions manager, noted that media interest in the

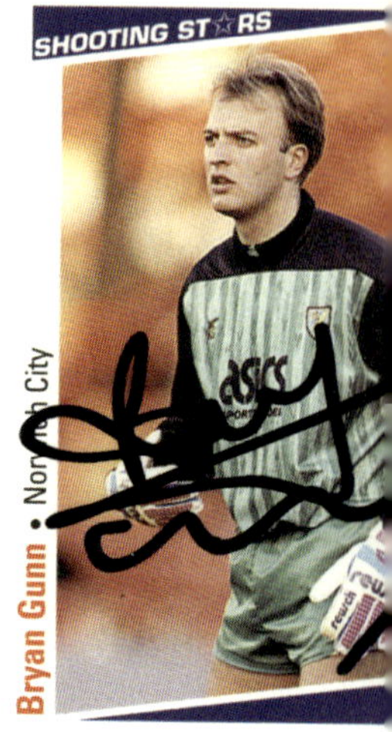

Player card
(Merlin Shooting Stars)
Author's collection

32 Bryan Gunn with Kevin Piper, *In Where It Hurts: My Autobiography* (Vision Sports, 2006), p. 202.

Player card (Topps)

Author's collection

club, including national double-page spreads and extensive television coverage, had made finding matchday sponsors much easier. The club's shirt sponsor, the Norwich & Peterborough Building Society, must also have been delighted. The yellow and green speckled shirt of the 1992/93 and 1993/94 seasons subsequently became a collectors' item.

Matthäus, a much-capped international and World Cup winner, had clearly not enjoyed Bayern's defeat in the first leg. Jeremy Goss has written that the German captain said that 'Norwich was a nothing little city, where the people just ate mustard.'[33] *I very much doubt that the Norwich City players or fans needed winding up for the return match, but that probably helped. The crowd on the night at Carrow Road in November 1993 was 20,829 – remarkably not the largest of the season, although that might have been down to there being fewer German visitors than might have been hoped for. Nevertheless, it would go down as one of the greatest matches in Norwich's history. It was certainly crowded in the South Stand where I had secured a ticket, and the expectation and the noise generated by the Norwich fans was intense, with inflatable 'Canaries into Europe' birds being waved to mark the occasion.*

There was an early goal for Bayern after less than five minutes from a corner, when Valencia bundled the ball in to level the tie. I have to confess that I expected the German side to score more then, as I imagine many other fans feared. In fact, Norwich held their own, and early in the second half came yet another memorable goal from Goss. Ruel Fox hung a long cross in that Chris Sutton flicked on at the near post for the Welsh midfielder to side foot in from close range. As Goss wrote later, 'I've never heard a crowd make as much noise as they did after that goal. I ran off, right arm in the air, screaming and screaming with joy.'[34] *Him and every one of the Canaries' fans that night at Carrow Road. With the final score remaining 1–1, Norwich had won 3–2 over the two legs. A truly remarkable victory against one of the European giants.*

In the next round, Norwich City drew another big name – FC Internazionale (Inter Milan). The photos from the game in the Eastern Evening News *show a good crowd who had flown over from Norwich Airport, including myself. Fans were taken direct to the stadium in*

33 Goss, *Gossy*, p. 124.

34 Ibid., p. 125.

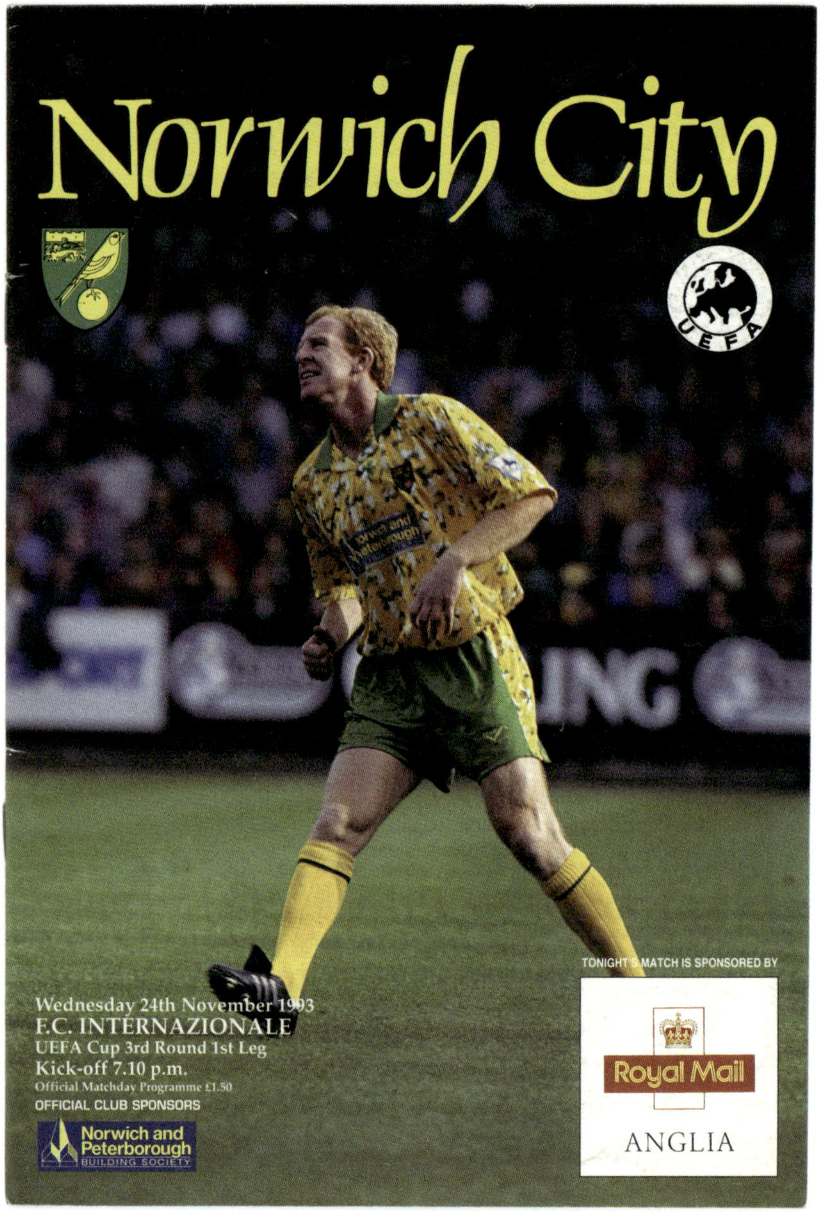

Front cover of match programme, Norwich City vs F.C. Internazionale, 24th November 1993

Author's collection

Norwich City Subbuteo team featuring the 'bird-poo' strip

Author's collection

772

NORWICH CITY

coaches – mine was under the direction of a smiling but firm Duncan Forbes no less. This time the occasion proved too much, with Denis Bergkamp scoring in both matches to send Norwich out 0–2 on aggregate. Chris Sutton recalled that Inter were simply too streetwise for Norwich and despite chances for both him and Ekoku in the second leg at the San Siro, the Norfolk club simply didn't play at their best. Years later, I went on a tour of the Italian ground and made sure I went into Inter's trophy room. I had not expected to find a reminder of the game anywhere, but there, in a corner in a large cabinet, was a ball from the game suitably identified. It wasn't just a dream then.

Today's clubs make a small fortune from just appearing in the Champions League, but that wasn't yet the case in European competition. Despite the increased income for the club, the money wasn't spent on new players as the fans wanted. By January 1994 Mike Walker had left for Everton, where no doubt he hoped his ambitions would be matched (ironically, he was dismissed by the Merseyside club just ten months later). The new manager, John Deehan, was obliged to sell Ruel Fox to Newcastle United for a club record of £2.25 million in February 1994, but this was surpassed just five months later in July, when Chris Sutton was bought by Blackburn Rovers for £5 million, a record fee for an English club. The purchase of defender Jon Newsome in June 1994, becoming the Canaries first million-pound player, was of scant solace to the fans. Efan Ekoku left for Wimbledon for another million in October. The most successful team in Norwich City's history was being dismantled.

Player card
(Merlin Collections)
Author's collection

Player card
(Merlin's Collections, Premier League 95 Collections)
Author's collection

Cool Britannia

At some point in the 1990s English football made a complete transformation, from the tragedies and the shabby and unsafe terraces of the 1980s, to become surprisingly and excitingly cool. Culture commentators will argue exactly when this happened.[35] It could have been Pavarotti belting out 'Nessun Dorma' on the BBC or John Barnes rapping to New Order's 'World in Motion'. It could have been Nick Hornby's middle-class depiction of the football fan in *Fever Pitch*. Tony Blair was certainly quick to catch on. His headers with Kevin Keegan during a visit to a leisure centre in Brighton in 1995 were heavily publicised.

35 Daniel Rachel, *Don't Look Back in Anger* (Trapeze, 2021).

Kevin Keegan and Tony Blair in 1995

PA Images / Alamy Stock Photo

Souvenir plate from EURO '96. The tournament helped the popularity of football in England as well as the European Championships themselves which were hosting 16 finalists for the first time. Liverpool was one of eight host cities. All stadiums used were refurbished after the Hillsborough Disaster. Indeed, Hillsborough provided one of the venues

Author's collection

Whilst George Best was football's first modern celebrity, the new Premier League needed glamorous and headline-grabbing stars if it was to become a complete entertainment television package. Just as Manchester United had provided Best in the 1960s, so the club produced Eric Cantona and David Beckham in the 1990s.[36] As money started to pour into the game, the media needed stories, ideally on the front as well as the back pages.

Manchester United were the first to monetise as many aspects of the game as they could. There's a lot of money to be made out of showbiz. Mihir Bose has discussed the 'marketing juggernaut' that Manchester United became in the 1990s.[37] Claude Boli describes the evolution of the club's business activities between 1961 and 2014, and this only accelerated with the coming of the Premier League.[38] Martin Edwards floated them on the stock market in 1991. In 1993 United launched a very popular *Manchester United Magazine* followed by a radio station in 1994; the club established a website in 1996 and then agreed a contract with HSBC Midland in 1997, which has a strong presence in Asia. The following year, United opened a museum, launched a TV channel and announced an increased capacity at Old Trafford. In 2000 the club opened three megastores – in Old Trafford, Singapore and Dublin. Bose noted that between 1991 and 1997, United's revenue rose from £17.8 million to £88 million. Similarly, Arsenal's increased from £15 million to £49 million between 1993 and 1999.[39] That's quite a difference.

Suddenly, English football was not only cool, it was also generating revenues that could not have been dreamt of in the very recent past. Norwich City, sadly, were never very cool or sexy. Supporters of clubs such as Derby County, Burnley, Preston North End and Huddersfield Town – despite their storied football histories – would probably admit the same with a shrug of the shoulders. Norwich is a lovely place to bring up a young family, but too far away from the swinging nightlife of London, Liverpool or Manchester. But in the early 90s at least, they were able to compete to some extent on the football field with the likes of Manchester United, Arsenal and Liverpool.

36 Ellis Cashmore, *Beckham* (Polity, 2002).

37 Mihir Bose, *Manchester Disunited: Trouble and Takeover at the World's Richest Football Club* (Aurum, 2007), p. 84.

38 Boli, 'Manchester United: the capitalized history', p. 409.

39 Kieran Maguire, *The Price of Football* (Agenda, 2020), p. 72.

Enter Delia

The second half of the 1990s proved a difficult time for Norwich City. Having enjoyed nine consecutive seasons at the top table of English football – still the club's most successful run – everything went downhill very fast after the departure of Mike Walker in January 1994. Remarkably for a club like Norwich, there were demonstrations against the chairman, Robert Chase. Fans were furious at a perceived lack of ambition as key players were sold. Whilst Chris Sutton felt that Chase did a good job in redeveloping Carrow Road, he also described the press conference where Chase said he would be open to offers for his striker when the player had already signed for Blackburn.[40] This followed the chairman's announcement at the start of the season that Sutton would not be going anywhere. Such duplicity never goes down well with fans!

Following a nasty injury to Norwich goalkeeper Bryan Gunn, in which he sustained a broken fibula and dislocated ankle during a 1–0 defeat to Nottingham Forest on 27 December 1994 when City were seventh in the table,[41] the club's descent was rapid. Mike Walker's replacement, John Deehan, resigned in April 1995. He was replaced by Gary Megson, who was unable to prevent Norwich's relegation to Division One (the new second league after the formation of the Premier League, which subsequently became the Championship in 2004) at the end of the 1994/95.

Only two years after nearly winning the Premier League, Norwich were consigned to the second level of English football and would not return for nine seasons. The financial hit was obvious. Norwich City's end-of-year accounts in 1993 showed an income of £7,117,000.[42] In 1999 income had gone down to £6,235,572.[43] The gap in revenue between the top two divisions in English football was growing at quite a rate.

Martin O'Neill's six-month stint as manager of Norwich City for the first half of the 1995/96 season is the source of many stories about the club. It is retold in O'Neill's own biography.[44] O'Neill had played for Norwich in 1980/81 under John Bond, and then again with Ken Brown, rejoining the club after spending six months at Manchester City. Chase argued that O'Neill never settled in Norfolk, but most other accounts say that it was the chairman's refusal to make money available for O'Neill to

40 Chris Sutton with Mark Guidi, *Paradise and Beyond: My Autobiography* (Black and White Publishing, 2011).

41 Woodrow, *Norwich City Football Club*, vol. III, 27 December 1994.

42 Ibid., vol. III, 4 September 1993.

43 Ibid., vol. III, 7 October 1999.

44 Alex Montgomery, *Martin O'Neill: The Biography* (Ted Smart, 2003).

bring new players in – specifically Hull City's Dean Windass – that led to the Irishman walking out of the door to go to Leicester City. Robert Chase was by now a hate figure amongst some supporters – there was a lively demonstration against him when four people were injured and 12 arrested in April 1995[45] and a further protest on Boxing Day that same year.[46] He finally departed in May 1996, having sold his shares to Geoffrey Watling.[47] Despite their very recent successes on the field, Norwich City were in a financial mess and in significant debt. Many other clubs, including Millwall and Bournemouth, were facing administration.

Michael Wynn-Jones and Delia Smith had been season-ticket holders since 1972. Their own fan journey coincided with Norwich City's first promotion to Division One, at exactly the same time I first visited Carrow Road. Wynn-Jones and Smith's interest-free loan in 1996 dug the club out of an immediate financial crisis, and Delia Smith joined the Norwich City board of directors, along with her husband, on 28 November 1996 (Michael Foulger and Barry Skipper were also appointed, having made similar long-term loans). A year later, Geoffrey Watling, a long-term follower and saviour of the club, sold his shareholding to Wynn-Jones and Smith. By 1998 the couple had become the majority shareholders.

Wynn-Jones and Smith in particular have always argued that they are custodians of the club and respect its key role in the community. In that sense, they perhaps represent the club owners of previous times. Similarly, like these owners, Wynn-Jones and Smith never sought to make money out of the club, and all the loans and cash they pumped into Norwich City over the years were always interest-free. But it would be wrong to portray them as unwilling to confront hard commercial truths.

It should also be remembered that Smith was and is primarily a celebrity cook. Her involvement with Norwich certainly fitted the mood of the times, although there were very few women involved in football at any senior level. Smith knew people in the fashion and cultural industries, and this helped the club in different ways. Meantime Smith and her husband did their best to develop Norwich City's commercial base: proposing a club shop in Castle Mall, finding new sponsors, and developing the club's catering operation – 'Delia's Canary Catering'. The latter began to generate new revenue for the club very swiftly.

45 Woodrow, *Norwich City Football Club*, vol. III, 29 April 1995.

46 Ibid., vol. III, 26 December 1995.

47 Ibid., vol. III, 2 May 1996.

Cutting the Mustard

The Norfolk-based mustard company Colman's (despite being bought up by Unilever in 1995) seemed the perfect new shirt sponsor for the new season in 1997, and certainly demonstrated Smith and Wynn-Jones' wish to modernise the club. The two-year contract with Norwich City was reported to be worth £250,000 a year.[48] Colman's had been manufacturing on its Carrow site in Norwich since 1858, and the brand (and the mustard) had become synonymous with the city – and they were past masters of advertising.[49] Indeed, the land at Carrow Road that Norwich City moved to in 1935 was owned by the Colman company, although then leased to the engineering firm of Boulton Paul. The club president, Russell Colman, cut a ribbon on 31 August in front of the main stand, whose roof carried a huge advert for Colman's mustard.

From the mid-1970s football shirts have been used to promote brands, and also functioned, increasingly, as replica merchandise. As already described, the advent of the Premier League helped to develop and accelerate all commercial aspects of the game. Fans were now consumers. Between the 1986/87 and the 1993/94 seasons, the proportion of fans wearing replica shirts increased from 3% to 30%.[50] The colour of team kits is very important to the tradition and heritage of football clubs and Norwich's own colours of yellow were adopted from their canary mascot in 1907.[51] Yellow has always been the predominant colour, with green trim featured in some way; green shorts were not introduced until 1965.[52]

Smith invited her friend, fashion designer Bruce Oldfield, to design a new strip for Norwich at the start of the 1997/98 season. Cameron Huggett describes perfectly how 'a combination of mustard and high fashion' won him over.[53] This after all was a high-fashion shirt when football was cool, and Oldfield had designed for celebrities and royalty alike. Football shirts were only just beginning to develop a replica kit industry, and this strip

48 Ibid., vol. III, 19 May 1997.

49 Roy Church and Christine Clark, 'The origins of competitive advantage in the marketing of branded packaged consumer goods: Colman's and Reckitt's in early Victorian Britain', in John F. Wilson, Ian Jones and Steven Toms (eds), *A Search for Competitive Advantage: Case Studies in Industrial History* (Routledge, 2021).

50 Alex Ireland, *Pretty Poly: The History of the Football Shirt* (Pitch Publishing, 2023).

51 An excellent description of the evolution of football shirts can be found in Christopher Stride, Jean Williams, David Moor and Nick Catley, 'From sportswear to leisurewear: the evolution of English Football League shirt design in the replica kit era', *Sport in History*, 35.1 (2014), pp. 156–94.

52 Roger Smith, *The Canary Companion* (RJS Publishing, 2004).

53 Cameron Huggett, 'My favourite Norwich shirt – 1997-1999 Home', *Along Come Norwich* (2022). Available at: https://www.alongcomenorwich.com/articles/my-favourite-norwich-shirt-1997-1999-home/ (accessed 14 May 2025).

Aerial Photograph of Carrow Road, c1935.

Courtesy Norfolk Record Office, ACC 1997/146/2/30, Boulton and Paul archive

In 1997, Norwich City's new shirt sponsor was Colman's with their new shirt designed by Bruce Oldfield

The 1997/98 version was controversially paired with yellow shorts

Collection of Alan Ward

Colman's
PONY

fulfilled the football shirt's requirement for authenticity, given the strong link between the mustard company and Norwich. As Huggett wrote:

> This is everything a sponsor should be, not some dubious betting company or multinational conglomerate using a football club as a billboard to shill something no one wants or needs. Colman's are as intertwined with the City of Norwich as the Canaries, and both club and brand have been instrumental in promoting the City to the world.[54]

Oldfield's 1997 design featured yellow shorts though, which proved controversial and unpopular. So much so that the club saw this as an opportunity to engage with their supporters and held roadshows with fans 'concerning the green shorts debate'. This culminated in a vote by the supporters before the home match against Bristol City in December 1998 which signalled a return to green.

Match Report: Saturday 9 August 1997, k/o 15:00.
Nationwide Football League Division One, Carrow Road,
Norwich City 0 Wolverhampton Wanderers 2. Attendance: 17,230.

Norwich City
Andy Marshall, Craig Fleming, Rob Newman (Craig Bellamy), Daryl Sutch, Victor Segura, John Polston, Neil Adams, Danny Mills, Iwan Roberts (Robert Fleck), Darren Eadie, Keith O'Neill. Manager: Mike Walker.

Wolverhampton Wanderers
Mike Stowell, Jamie Smith, Dariusz Kubicki, Mark Atkins, Steve Sedgley, Keith Curle, Darren Ferguson, Robbie Keane, Steve Bull, Don Goodman, Steve Froggatt. Manager: Mark McGhee.

Goals
Wolverhampton Wanderers: Keane (34, 56)

The opening match of every new season always brings excitement and expectation. Norwich had faced down a very challenging time in 1996, with its financial burdens impacting on all areas of its operation. Bringing Delia Smith and Michael Wynn-Jones on to the board was essential to keep the club alive, but it was also, remarkably, the beginning of a twenty-eight-year period of their proprietorship of the club (although they did not acquire majority ownership until 1998).

54 Ibid.

Excerpt from the Norwich City vs Bristol City matchday programme, 19th December 1998 (page 5)
Author's collection

Shorts Vote . . . . Shorts Vote . . . Shorts Vote . . . . Shorts Vote

YELLOW OR GREEN

you decide

Todays game will be preceded by a ballot, which we feel is quite unprecedented in British football.

It isn't unusual to see fans use placards to get their feelings across, but this is most usually when they are spontaneously demonstrating over an issue. Most recently, fans of Leicester City held up signs urging Martin O'Neill not to join Leeds United. Red cards have frequently been used when fans launch a protest. Visually, this can present a powerful case. However, it is most uncommon, indeed has probably never happened before, that a CLUB has offered fans the chance to have their say. Indeed, a chance in front of the glare of the media, on a matchday, when thousands of fans come together in the one place.

The issue of green shorts, or what the Pink-Un calls the lack of them (!) is being put to the vote. One of the assets this club has is that it does listen to its fans. Not only that, it commits time and money to do so - witness the 16 Roadshows that have been held all over the County.

Today, at each home turnstile, each fan will be issued with a double sided card; yellow on one side, green on the other. There will be a chance at about ten to three, to raise the card above your head, not forgetting that if you want to vote green, then green must face the pitch. To vote for yellow, turn the card such that yellow faces the pitch. Sorry if that is stating the obvious, but there is no room for "spoilt papers" or void votes!

The media have latched on to the green shorts debate, and have responded well to the notion of this unique referendum. So please take part, and make sure that you are part of making history.

To help ensure that we keep Carrow Road as tidy as possible, could you please take your card home with you. I would have thought anyway that most people would want to keep their card as a reminder of the day that thousands of fans took part in a club issue.

By the way, the FURTHER issue as to whether you can change kit mid season, having registered the kits at the start is covered under the F.A Laws of the game. I rang to seek clarification on Wednesday morning....Ooops bad day for the F.A!

Steve Greenall

This was the 1999-2001 shirt, as shown on a pin badge. The shorts were green once again
Author's collection

Front cover of match programme, Norwich City vs Wolverhampton Wanderers, 9th August 1997

Author's collection

Player signed photo

Author's collection

The reappointment of Mike Walker in June 1996 certainly symbolised a hoped-for return of past glories, whilst the departure of club heroes Mark Bowen and Jeremy Goss over this season indicated that a rebuilding of the Norwich City squad was required. Craig Bellamy, a young and exciting prospect, was given his first-team debut towards the end of the 1996/97 season, in which Norwich finished a disappointing 13th in Division One.

The summer of 1997 saw the further rebuilding of the squad. Walker bought Craig Fleming from Oldham, and Iwan Roberts signed from Wolves for £900,000. Roberts would admit himself that he wasn't in the best physical condition when he first arrived at Carrow Road, and it would take another season for the striker to find his form. A Spanish defender, Victor Segura, also joined the club.

After the turmoil and downright anger at the end of Robert Chase's time at Norwich City, the new board did its best to improve communications with the fans, with regular Supporter Forums and a Supporters' Consultative Group.[55] *The programme for the match against Wolves also demonstrated the club's attempts to develop their commercial model. The inside front cover features Colman's Question of Sport: 'How hot are you on the Canaries?' (Keen as Mustard?). On page 6, the News Desk has a column entitled 'Internet launched'. A new site was announced on the World Wide Web at www.ecn.co.uk/ncfc/. The site was developed with Eastern Counties Network, the publishing arm of the* Pink 'Un, Evening News *and* Eastern Daily Press. *It was the first time the club had been directly involved in a website. The website promised to provide information on the club along with full player profiles and statistics. Like other innovations in information technology though, the site would be developed to draw in more fans and increase consumption of the club's (and its partnering sponsors') products. The real benefit to the club was clearly laid out by Will Hoy, Norwich City's brand development manager, in the match programme for a pre-season friendly with Leicester City on 28 July 2001, in describing a new agreement for the website with NTL: 'in the first year, the Club has already received over £500,000. The amount of money we make all depends upon how successful the site is. It's as simple as that. The busier the site is, the more money Norwich*

55 Mike Davage, John Eastwood and Kevan Platt, *Canary Citizens: Centenary Edition* (Jarrold Publishing, 2002).

City Football Club will make.' Some examples of the club's new leisure wear were advertised later in the Wolves match programme. A 'V-Neck Collared Line Collection Shirt' was available for purchase for £17.99, for example.

Wolves had just missed out on promotion from Division One the preceding season, having lost their play-off semi-final to Crystal Palace (who went on to be promoted). The Wolves forward line was formidable indeed, featuring the Black Country legend Steve Bull, Don Goodman and Robbie Keane, the latter making his league debut. The Norwich line-up included their new signings, Fleming and Roberts, with Craig Bellamy coming on as a sub in the second half. It was Keane who hit the headlines though. He scored twice, one in each half, in front of a 17,230 crowd at Carrow Road, leaving Wolves 2–0 victors. The first was a volley which left the goalkeeper, Andy Marshall, completely flatfooted. In the second half, Keane waltzed past Segura and the Norwich defence to toe-poke the winner past Marshall. It was a dispiriting start and, indeed, Norwich were bottom of the table after the first three matches.

Craig Bellamy made 38 appearances and scored 13 goals in what turned out to be another underwhelming season for the Canaries. Bellamy reflected on this time in his autobiography, in a statement that could be repeated at other times by other players during Norwich City's on-off relationship with the Premier League:

'The optimism around the club had died but perhaps in a way that helped me. Maybe if the club had been pressing for promotion, first team opportunities for someone like me would have been limited but Norwich had been plunged into a financial crisis as it tried to adapt to no longer being in the Premier League and as a result, young lads like me were getting a chance'.[56]

Although Norwich did improve in 1997/98, going on to finish 15th, it was the end of the road for Mike Walker. The 'Messiah' was not able to deliver on a second occasion and he left the club 'by mutual consent'. The new managerial team were duly announced as Bruce Rioch and Bryan Hamilton. Sadly, Bellamy's own time with Norwich was also limited, as a dangerous tackle by defender Kevin Muscat in another

56 Craig Bellamy with Oliver Holt, *Good Fella: An Autobiography* (Sport Media, 2014), p. 70.

game with Wolves in December 1998 left him seriously injured until the end of the 1999/2000 season. By the time he was fully recovered, the club had accepted an offer from Coventry City for £6.5 million and another exceptional talent had left the club's books. Bellamy followed Darren Eadie, who had been sold to Leicester City for £3 million in December 1999.

Off the Box and Out of Sight

Among the few positives from the 1997/98 season on the pitch – ironically resulting from injury problems – was the blooding of youngsters such as Adrian Forbes, Darren Kenton and Craig Bellamy. A smaller club's lifeline of developing young players before inevitably selling them on to bigger clubs was already self-evident.

For Delia Smith and Michael Wynn-Jones, the reality of running a club outside the Premier League was becoming abundantly clear. As Wynn-Jones has said, 'Running a football club, we very soon discovered, is like running no other business in the world: conventional models go out of the window.'[57] They would be tested both then and in the future regarding what they believed would be the best way forward for the club.

The truth at the end of the 90s was that Norwich City found themselves marooned outside the Premier League, which was already developing commercially at an amazing speed. The first broadcasting rights package which had been signed with BSkyB for £190 million in 1992 had been replaced by a new deal for £670 million in 1997.[58] The money was flowing, but Norwich City were off the telly and out of sight.

57 Michael Wynn-Jones, 'Recollections from the River End and elsewhere', in Mick Dennis (ed.), *Tales from the City, Volume One: A Collection of Writing about Norwich City Football Club* (Tales From, 2015), p. 39.

58 Tom Evens, Petros Iosifidis and Paul Smith, *The Political Economy of Television Sports Rights* (Palgrave Macmillan, 2013).

flybe.com

THE 2000s

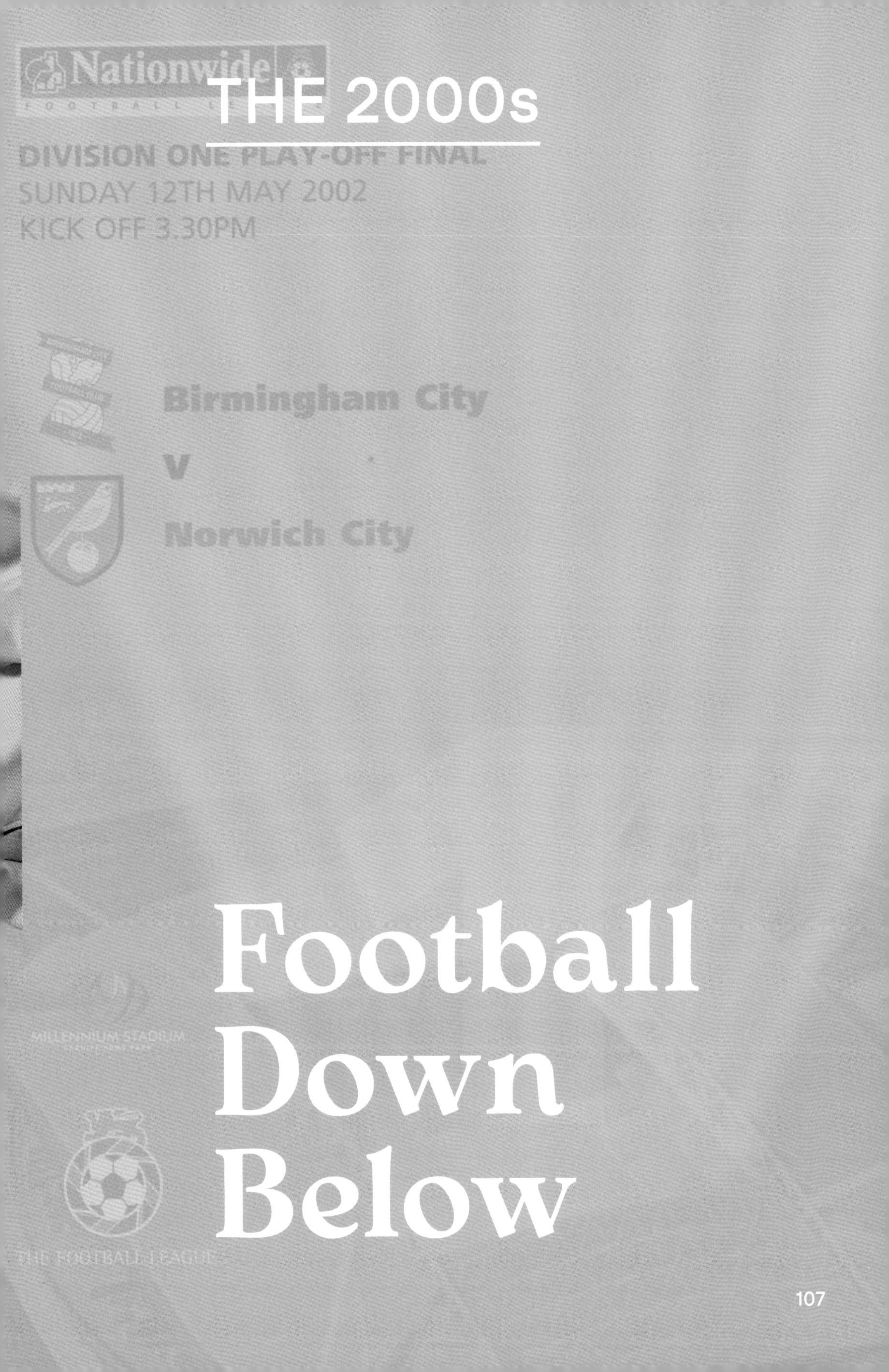

Football Down Below

Football Down Below

2001 Re-election of Tony Blair as UK Prime Minister; attack on World Trade Center, New York (9/11); US/UK invasion of Afghanistan

2002 Fulham FC are the first EPL club to have a gambling brand (Betfair) on the front of their shirt; British parliament passes legislation banning tobacco advertising (including sponsorship); the demolition of Wembley Stadium commences

2003 Manchester City move into the City of Manchester Stadium (now the Etihad), the site of the Commonwealth Games in 2002; Roman Abramovich buys Chelsea FC for £140m; US invasion of Iraq

2004 Facebook launched; rebranding of the Football League competitions; the FA introduce the Owners' and Directors' Test to combat corruption; Lehman Brothers establishes its European headquarters in Canary Wharf

2005 Tony Blair wins third term as UK Prime Minister; Malcolm Glazer takes a controlling interest in Manchester United; YouTube established; UK Gambling Act passed

2006 Arsenal move into their new Emirates Stadium; Twitter set up

2007 Blair resigns as Prime Minister in June and is replaced by Gordon Brown; launch of iPhone; European Commission rule that Sky's monopoly of EPL coverage in the UK is not in the interest of the consumer; the new Wembley Stadium opens

2007–2008 Global financial crisis

2008 Manchester City taken over by Sheikh Mansour bin Zayed al Nahyan through the Abu Dhabi United Group in August; Instagram established

Previous spread: Flybe sponsored Norwich City for two seasons, from 2006 to 2008. Background: cover of the match programme of the Division One Play-Off Final, 12th May 2002

Author's collections

Foreign Takeovers and Financial Crises

Financial journalist Alex Brummer estimates that in the eighteen years of Conservative government from 1979 to 1997, over £60 billion of UK business assets were transferred to the private sector from the state.[1] The Labour governments of the first decade maintained very similar policies, with waves of privatisations and private-sector interests welcomed in both the education and health sectors, for example.[2] Even as British manufacturing assets were being disposed of, London was establishing itself as a financial centre. In 2000 alone, America's CitiGroup bought Schroders investment banking arm, and Chase Manhattan Bank obtained Robert Fleming & Co., another investment bank. Similarly, Courtaulds Textiles was sold to Sara Lee of the USA; the mobile phone operator Orange was sold to France Telecom; and Thames Water was acquired by the German company RWE.[3] So it was no great surprise when the Russian oligarch Roman Abramovich bought Chelsea FC for £140 million in 2003. As James Montague wrote, this was a transformational moment in football: clubs wanting to compete with Chelsea now had to find comparable sources of income.[4]

Brummer argued that in the post-9/11 era, in a period of low interest rates, companies expanded through borrowing, using 'gearing' to fund business takeovers. He gave the example of Debenhams, which was bought by US-based private equity firms in 2003 and was then stripped of cash and investment. In 2005 the Florida-based Glazer family bought Manchester United for £800 million in another highly leveraged purchase. Liverpool FC was next – in 2007 – sold to another US consortium for £285 million. And in 2008, with a stadium inherited from the Manchester Commonwealth Games, Manchester City was sold to an Abu Dhabi group, which in turn had bought the club from its previous Thai investor. Whilst all these foreign takeovers have at least left the clubs successful on the football field (with the arguable exception of Manchester United), the Indian Venkey Group's takeover of Blackburn Rovers (2010) and Carson Yeung's (Hong Kong) purchase of Birmingham City (2009) were less productive.

The Blair government's embrace of free-market policies led to the Gambling Act of 2005, which completely changed football's relationship with the gambling industry. Whilst Fulham had the first gambling sponsor

1 Alex Brummer, *Britain for Sale: British Companies in Foreign Hands – The Hidden Threat to our Economy* (Random House, 2012).

2 Simon Jenkins, *Thatcher & Sons: A Revolution in Three Acts* (Allen Lane, 2006).

3 Brummer, *Britain for Sale.*

4 James Montague, *The Billionaires Club: The Unstoppable Rise of Football's Super-rich Owners* (Bloomsbury Sport, 2018).

(Betfair in 2002/03), the new Act significantly liberalised gambling laws and enabled gambling companies to advertise on our television screens.[5] With the accompanying development of online gambling, gambling brands began to be seen whenever we watched football.[6] It wasn't only the brands on the front of shirts, we now saw bookies advertising on pitch perimeters. And as social media platforms grew, so fans were encouraged to bet on all aspects of the game.

However, the crisis in 2007 at Northern Rock – the shirt sponsors of Newcastle United FC – showed that a financial sector based on borrowing and debt was not as stable as the Labour government had hoped. The bankruptcy of Lehman Brothers in September was a nail in this particular coffin. Brown and his chancellor Alistair Darling's solution was to inject equity from the state into the banks;[7] the football business developed in a similar way in the 1990s and 2000s. But building debt as a way of financing short-term success meant that crisis was never far away, particularly for clubs like Norwich City, which spent most of the decade in what in 2005 had been rebranded as the Championship, but which continuously sought elevation to the TV glare and riches of the Premier League.

Beyond the Bright Lights

2001/02 marked Norwich City's seventh successive season in the second tier of English football. The club was suffering from a much-reduced income compared to the big boys in the Premier League and the lack of screen exposure meant it was harder to attract sponsors. In 2001 the Norfolk-based Digital Phone Company (DPC) became Norwich City's sixth shirt sponsor. Five of these first six sponsors were associated with Norwich or Norfolk in some way – Poll Withey Windows (1983–86), Norwich Breweries (Foster's lager) (1986–89), Norwich & Peterborough Building Society (1992–97), Colman's (1997–2001), and now DPC. DPC began trading in Great Yarmouth in 1994 and sponsored Norwich City in order to integrate themselves into local communities and support local businesses. It is always easier for a club such as Norwich City to find local sponsors who then use their association with the club to drive their business forward and bring in new consumers.

5 Christopher Bunn, Robin Ireland, Jonathan Minton et al., 'Shirt sponsorship by gambling companies in the English and Scottish Premier Leagues: global reach and public health concerns', *Soccer & Society*, 20.6 (2019), pp. 824–35.

6 Rob Davies, *Jackpot: How Gambling Conquered Britain* (Guardian Faber, 2022).

7 Steve Richards, *Turning Points: Crisis and Change in Modern Britain from 1945 to Truss* (Macmillan, 2023).

Digital phone company. 'On the call with City'. Taken from match programme in 2001/02 season

Author's collection

By this time the club's sponsorship sales manager was former goalkeeper and club legend Bryan Gunn. It was a role Gunn held for seven years, which enabled Norwich to benefit from his connection to their heritage as well as bringing more commercial success. In 'Gunny & Gossy's Sponsorship Round-up' column in the programme produced for City's first Nationwide Division One match of the 2001/02 against Kevin Keegan's Manchester City (the Canaries won 2–0 although Manchester City went on to be the league champions), Gunny welcomed the new sponsor. A few years later, the *Great Yarmouth Mercury* reported that the Digital Phone Company had provided the biggest shirt sponsorship deal in the Canaries' 99-year history (although not providing any figures as to its value). At the time, fans were offered a customised Norwich City mobile phone (in home and away colours), complete with an 'On the Ball, City' ringtone.[8]

Shirt produced for 2002/03 centenary. Sponsorship from the Digital Phone Company
Author's collection

In the second year of DPC's shirt sponsorship, Norwich produced a shirt to mark the club's centenary. The blue and white colours matched the blue and white halves that the club wore between 1902 and 1907, only adopting yellow shirts in 1907. The home shirt remained yellow in 2002/03, but in a nod to tradition, the special edition blue and white shirt even carried supporters' names.

City's sponsorship fee would have been much less than that received by the larger clubs in the Premier League, who could secure deals with companies and brands seeking larger and often global audiences. Thus, in the period of DPC's sponsorship of Norwich, Liverpool were sponsored by Carlsberg and Manchester United by Vodafone.

Bryan Gunn and his wife, who lost their young daughter to leukaemia in 1992, have been involved in fundraising to combat the disease ever since. The City of Norwich recognised Gunn for his charitable work in Norwich City's centenary year in 2002, by making him Sheriff of Norwich.

On the Ball, City!

A club's tradition and heritage need to be protected at all costs. When Malaysian investor Vincent Tan completed his takeover of Cardiff City in 2012, he changed the team colours from blue to red, as red is considered lucky in some parts of Asia.[9] Hardly surprisingly, the change did not go down well with Cardiff's supporters (the team reverted back to its traditional blue in 2015). Norwich City's decision to change to yellow shorts in 1998 only lasted one season as fans demanded the more traditional green.

8 'Bryan Gunn's new Great Yarmouth job', *Great Yarmouth Mercury*, 6 November 2009. Available at: https://www.greatyarmouthmercury.co.uk/news/21041015.bryan-gunns-new-great-yarmouth-job/ (accessed 14 May 2025).

9 'Cardiff City FC owner on changing club colours to red', BBC news, 14 June 2012. Available at: https://www.bbc.co.uk/news/uk-wales-south-east-wales-18448754 (accessed 14 May 2025).

DPC
Digital Phone Company
XARA

Every club is proud of its origin story and Norwich City's is well told in *Canary Citizens*, which was produced to mark the club's centenary.[10] As the book describes, the club was formed at a meeting at the Criterion Café in White Lion Street, Norwich, on 17 June 1902. The day was celebrated in June 2002 when the formation of the Norwich City Football Club Historical Trust was announced.[11] Norwich City played their first match on Newmarket Road on 6 September in a friendly against Harwich & Parkeston, which they drew 1–1.

Songs are a key part of every team's history, and Norwich City's 'On the Ball, City' is the longest team chant on record.[12] Originally composed in the 1890s, and thus unlike any other songs heard on terraces today, it is still being sung at Carrow Road. As Andrew Lawn writes, 'the song features none of the tub-thumping one-upmanship which characterises many modern chants and instead focuses fully on the club and the sense of hope, joy and community fostered by the collective playing of sport'.[13]

Kick it off, throw it in, have a little scrimmage,
Keep it low, a splendid rush, bravo, win or die;
On the ball, City, never mind the danger,
Steady on, now's your chance,
Hurrah, we've scored a goal,
City, City, City (chorus).

Tradition and authenticity are key components of English football and clubs tread a fine line between respecting their history whilst seeking to exploit it. Indeed, the whole traditional experience of attending a live match has largely been replaced by an entertainment product made in a television studio that is intended for a viewer and, it can be argued, a potential consumer of the advertising which accompanies the match package.[14]

Wembley Stadium

Tradition and heritage were clearly at the heart of the Football Association's decision to rebuild Wembley Stadium on the site of the stadium that had been built for the British Empire Exhibition of 1924. The old Wembley

10 Mike Davage, John Eastwood and Kevan Platt, *Canary Citizens: Centenary Edition. The Official History of Norwich City F.C.* (Jarrold Publishing, 2002).

11 James Woodrow (as compiled for the Norwich City Football Club), *Norwich City Football Club: The Archive* (Severn, 2022), vol. IV, 17 June 2002.

12 Andrew Lawn, *We Lose Every Week – The History of Football Chanting* (Ockley Books, 2020).

13 Ibid., p. 35.

14 Roland Robertson, *Globalization: Social Theory and Global Culture* (Sage, 1992).

was the venue for the 1948 Olympic Games, and it was where England won the World Cup in 1966. There was a strong debate at the time as to whether there should be a Wembley of the North to replace the original stadium, but eventually, in 1996, the decision was made to build the new stadium on the original site.

However, the new Wembley was constructed to reflect the needs of a modern stadium where all parts are commodified, including its advertising hoardings, its ratio of cheap seats to corporate boxes, and its food and drink franchises. Architectural author Benjamin S. Flowers describes how 'Sporting spaces operate as a machine for spending',[15] and Wembley was designed to extract every coin possible.

This also applies to the events taking place there. The FA's business plan for developing Wembley included the staging of the FA Cup Final and international matches for at least twenty-five years.[16] Demolition of the old stadium began in 2002 and the new stadium reopened for the FA Cup Final on 19 May 2007. Since 2008 the new Wembley Stadium has also staged the FA Cup semi-finals, which previously would have been contested at neutral venues closer to home. This financial commitment has led to situations where fans of two northern clubs have had to travel to London to see a match when previously Villa Park or Hillsborough might have been used. With kick-off times determined by television coverage, supporters have sometimes not been able to catch their train home to the north of England after late finishing matches. So money was now being prioritised before fans.

Pin badges produced for 2002/03 centenary
Author's collection

15 Benjamin S. Flowers, *Sport and Architecture* (Routledge, 2017), p. 37.

16 Patrick Barclay and Kenneth Powell, *Wembley Stadium: Venue of Legends* (Prestel, 2007).

Match Report: Sunday 12 May 2002, k/o 15:30.
Division One Play-Off Final, Millennium Stadium, Cardiff,
Norwich City 1 Birmingham City 1 after extra time
(Birmingham City won 4–2 on penalties). Attendance: 71,597

Norwich City
Robert Green, Darren Kenton, Adam Drury, Malky Mackay, Craig Fleming, Philip Mulryne, Gary Holt, David Nielsen (Iwan Roberts), Paul McVeigh (Daryl Sutch), Mark Rivers (Alex Notman), Clint Easton. Manager: Nigel Worthington.

Birmingham City
Nico Vaesen, Jeff Kenna, Michael Johnson, Steve Vickers (Darren Carter), Martin Grainger, Paul Devlin, Bryan Hughes, Olivier Tébily, Tommy Mooney (Stan Lazaridis), Geoff Horsfield (Andrew Johnson), Stern John. Manager: Steve Bruce

Goals
Norwich City: Roberts (91)
Birmingham City: Horsfield (102)

Norwich City had not entered the new millennium with a fanfare. Another star player was sold to make ends meet when Darren Eadie was bought by Leicester City for £3 million. This had followed reports of increased debts, with a reported annual loss for the year to 30 June 1999 of £2.5 million.[17] *Manager Bruce Rioch left in March 2000 to be replaced by Bryan Hamilton. A distinctly average season in the Nationwide Football League Division One (Norwich finished 12th in 1999/2000) was followed by a poor start to 2000/01, with another star player, Craig Bellamy, leaving for big money. Free transfer stars brought in from Leicester City, Tony Cottee and Steve Walsh, proved not to be a success. Scott Parker also arrived on a one-month loan in October 2000. Two months later Hamilton resigned on 4 December after a bruising 2–0 defeat at Portsmouth left City at 20th in the league. The then assistant manager, Nigel Worthington, was placed in charge. The club finished 15th in the final table, and Worthington embarked on some serious rebuilding to prepare for the new season. In March 2001 the manager had already brought in Gary Holt from Kilmarnock, and Adam Drury from Peterborough United. In June Clint Easton and Mark Rivers had joined them, and Neil Emblen (Wolverhampton Wanderers) and Marc Libbra (Toulouse) followed a month later.*

17 Davage, Eastwood and Platt, *Canary Citizens: Centenary Edition.*

Cover of the match programme of the Division One Play-Off Final, 12th May 2002

Author's collection

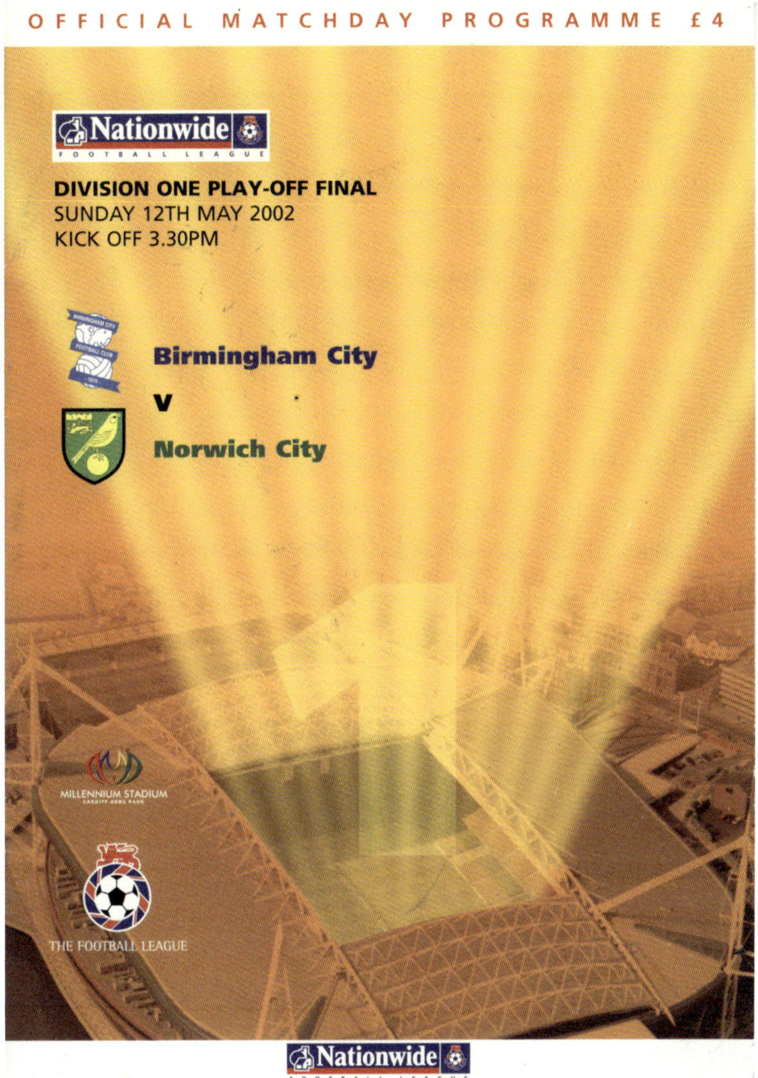

Match day ticket for the Division One Play-Off Final, 12th May 2002

Author's collection

Norwich started 2001/02 with an away defeat by 4–0 to Millwall. Things could only get better. The programme for the club's opening home fixture against Manchester City indicated the club's continued efforts to increase their income, including a Golden Goal ticket featuring a scratch card in which you hoped the two times specific to your ticket would match the goal times. Well, it all helps. In fact, things got a whole lot better. By November, when Norwich were at home to Bradford City, they were second in the Nationwide League Division One and looking forward to Christmas. The Football League had agreed a £315 million three-year deal with ITV Digital in June 2000, and finances were looking good, with 88 live Nationwide League and Worthington Cup (the latest incarnation of the League Cup) matches being shown in 2001/02. The end-of-year accounts for June 2001 showed a £9.4 million income (up from £7.7 million the previous year), largely due to increased TV money and the club's internet deal.[18]

Bryan Gunn and his fellow Canary legend Jeremy Goss had their own two-page spread in the Bradford match programme describing how your company could support the club. Martin Reynolds Construction sponsored the match against Wolves whilst Bennetts Electrical sponsored the match ball. Delia's Canary Catering was also doing excellent business with special events, 'Traditional Christmas Party Nights' and meals in Delia's City Brasserie. Bryan Gunn had even purchased a winning Golden Goal ticket. The Canary Store in Castle Mall was stocked high with Christmas gift ideas. ITV Digital showed Norwich's average attendances at 19,015.

Norwich went on to lose 1–4 to Bradford in November, however, and their form continued to slip, with losses to Stockport, Birmingham City (4–0) and Nottingham Forest before the turn of the year. Meantime David Nielsen was signed on an initial one-month loan from Wimbledon on 14 December (a fee of £210,000 was agreed when the signing was confirmed in January 2002). When Birmingham completed the double over City at Carrow Road on 15 March, after Gary Holt's penalty was saved by Nico Vaesen, Norwich had slipped to 10th place with 58 points. Against Gillingham, just a few days later, it was Phil Mulryne's turn to miss a spot-kick, but nevertheless Norwich came back from losing 1–0

18 Woodrow, *Norwich City Football Club*, vol. III, 13 November 2001.

at half-time to win 2–1 with goals from Clint Easton and Darron Kenton. When the Canaries went to Barnsley's Oakwell Stadium in April, they were on an unbeaten run of six matches but had to win against the Yorkshire club and at home to Stockport to secure a place in the top six. Goals from David Nielsen and Paul McVeigh secured the necessary win at Barnsley, but Norwich still had to better Burnley's result to grab a play-off place in the final game of the season on 21 April. This time it was Mulryne (though this is sometimes recorded as an own goal) and Malky Mackay who got the goals after Stockport's goalkeeper, Andy Dibble, had been sent off in the first minute. I remember listening on the radio as one Paul Gascoigne had a late free-kick chance for Burnley, which would have put the Lancashire team above the Canaries. In the end, Norwich's late charge to gain sixth place – one place and one point behind Birmingham City – left them in the play-offs with a goal difference of +9 (Burnley had +8) on 75 points (Manchester City strolled the Championship that season with 99 points).

The play-off system had been introduced in 1986/87 to try and increase football attendances by bringing excitement to the end of the football season. And whilst in 2002 the Division One play-off final was not yet hyped as the richest game in club football, the match programme described it as a £30 million ticket to the Premiership. In order to reach the final, though, Norwich had to overcome Wolverhampton Wanderers, who had narrowly missed out on an automatic promotion place by finishing third, three points behind local rivals West Bromwich Albion, but still 11 points in front of Norwich. Wolves were the firm favourites, but despite taking the lead in a tumultuous first leg at Carrow Road, goals from Rivers, McVeigh and a last-minute header from Mackay gave the Canaries a 3–1 lead to take to Molineux. The Black Country team could only get one goal back in the return leg despite huge pressure in the final minutes. After their hard battle to the play-offs, perhaps Nigel Worthington's men thought it was going to be their day.

With the original Wembley now being demolished, the match was played at the Millennium Stadium, Cardiff. It was my first ever visit to the Welsh capital. The weather was superb, and the city centre was full of yellow and green (and blue and white to be fair). This was Norwich's first showing in the play-offs, and to say I was excited would be a huge understatement. After all it was seven years since the Canaries had been in the Premier League following their dramatic fall from grace after those heady early years in the top division.

Birmingham City featured Belgian Nico Vaesen in goal, Darren Purse and Jeff Kenna in defence, with Stern John and Geoff Horsfield leading the attack. Birmingham's manager Steve Bruce and their coach, Mark Bowen, were both former Norwich heroes. The Canaries' starting line-up included Robert Green in goal, Adam Drury, Craig Fleming, Malky Mackay, Gary Holt and Paul McVeigh. The atmosphere was electric with the stadium roof closed because of the sunny weather (really!), and Atomic Kitten provided pre-match entertainment.

Norwich's top scorer Iwan Roberts had been injured and was on the bench before coming on in the 82nd minute. The match finished 0–0 after 90 minutes, with the high excitement coming in extra time. Roberts put Norwich ahead 40 seconds after the restart with a great header from an Alex Notman cross. In some previous matches this would have won the match on the 'golden goal rule' and the Welshman clearly thought it had. He later recalled, 'after getting off the floor after celebrating with the lads I turned around and realised Stern John and Geoff Horsfield were ready to restart the game. We obviously weren't using the golden goal!'[19]

However, this match could only be concluded after the full 30 minutes of extra time and Geoff Horsfield headed an equaliser for Birmingham towards the end of the first half. The match went to a penalty shootout. Rick Waghorn of the Eastern Evening News *had noted that Norwich had missed their last three penalties in the season. And sure enough, Norwich missed two of their penalties (Mulryne and Sutch) whilst Birmingham scored all of theirs. City had fallen agonisingly short at the final hurdle.*

I remember running to the railway station after the game in a desperate (and failed) effort to make a swift exit. I bumped into an old Norwich mate in my rush. He had brought his four small sons to the game. God knows how they all dealt with it!

Nigel Worthington knew immediately the financial impact of those missed penalties: 'If we had been promoted we would have had money to spend but now we might end up looking for Bosman signings.'[20]

19 Iwan Roberts, 'Not the worst, after all', in Mick Dennis (ed.), *Tales from the City, Volume One: A Collection of Writing about Norwich City Football Club* (Tales From, 2015), p. 59.

20 Chris Lakey, 'Do you remember Norwich City's 2002 play-off final against Birmingham?', *PinkUn*, 28 January 2023. Available at: https://www.pinkun.com/news/23279196.remember-norwich-citys-2002-play-off-final-birmingham/ (accessed 14 May 2025).

Digital Debacles

Norwich City's footballing failure at the Millennium Stadium was swiftly followed by some devastating financial news for both the Canaries and all other teams in the Football League. ITV Digital, originally ONdigital, was a British digital terrestrial television broadcaster which launched a pay-TV service in competition with Sky Digital. ONdigital, co-owned by ITV companies Carlton and Granada, had agreed to a £315 million deal with the Football League to show live matches. The contract had been announced in June 2000 and Norwich City estimated a resultant income of around £2.7 million per season; the previous deal with Sky Television had been worth about £700,000 per season.[21]

Quite simply, the ITV Digital service bombed. By January 2001 the service had one million subscribers whilst Sky Digital had 5.7 million. People preferred to pay for their services via Sky's satellite dishes than through conventional aerials.[22] It was felt at the time that Sky had refused to put ITV Sport on its channel list as that would be giving away its power in the football broadcasting world.

The writing was on the wall. By March 2002 it was reported that ITV Digital were proposing to make a huge reduction on the remaining two years of their Football League deal. In the match programme for the Norwich vs Birmingham play-off final, David Burns, chief executive of the Football League, wrote of the League's ongoing dispute with Carlton Communications and Granada, 'These two major UK companies with a combined value of over £5 billion, continue to refuse the obligations that they freely entered into with their clubs, in pursuit of profits for faceless shareholders and institutions.' ITV Digital was finally liquidated in April 2002, with only £135 million paid to the Football League.[23] Keith Harris, the Football League chairman, said that the loss of the League's court case against the ITV companies would put the future of dozens of clubs into doubt.

BSkyB immediately bought the rights to broadcast Football League matches for a reported £95 million over the next four seasons (2003 to 2006). Many Football League clubs, including Norwich, endured financial hardship as a result of the loss of expected broadcasting revenues.

21 Woodrow, *Norwich City Football Club*, vol. III, 18 June 2000.

22 'Granada urged to ditch ONdigital', BBC news, 27 June 2001. Available at: http://news.bbc.co.uk/1/hi/business/1409758.stm (accessed 14 May 2025).

23 Stephen Dobson and John Goddard, *The Economics of Football (Second Edition)* (Cambridge University Press, 2011).

At the beginning of the 2002/03 season, Joe Ferrari, Norwich City's public relations manager, wrote that the ITV Digital debacle had left the club with a £4 million hole to fill over the next two seasons and that some clubs could even cease to exist as a result of this loss in revenue.[24] Like every other Football League club, Norwich were left scrabbling to raise cash from every means. Delia's Canary Catering was doing just that. In 2001, after eleven months of trading, they had made a £681,000 profit for the club as well as undoubtedly improving the quality of the food served up at Carrow Road.

Delia Smith was vocal in her criticism of Carlton Communications and Granada

PA Images / Alamy Stock Photo

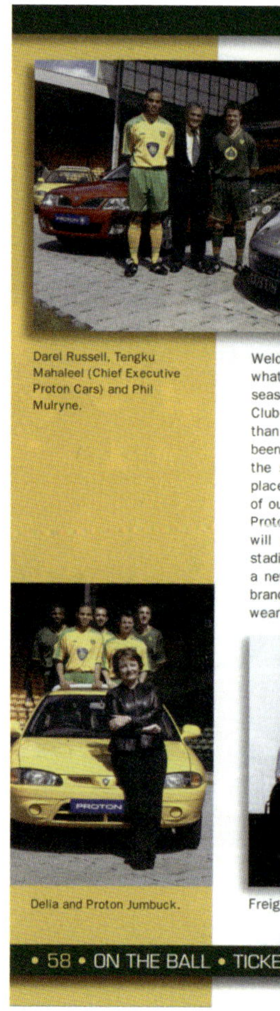

The sponsorship agreement was announced in the match programme produced for the pre-season friendly with Tottenham Hotspur on 22nd July 2003. The piece featured 'Delia and Proton Jumbuck'

Author's collection

24 Joe Ferrari, 'City Diary', in *On the Ball*, Norwich City vs Grimsby Town match programme, 10 August 2002.

Match Report: Saturday 3 April 2004, k/o 15:00.
Nationwide Division One, Turf Moor, Burnley 3 Norwich City 5.
Attendance: 12,417.[25]

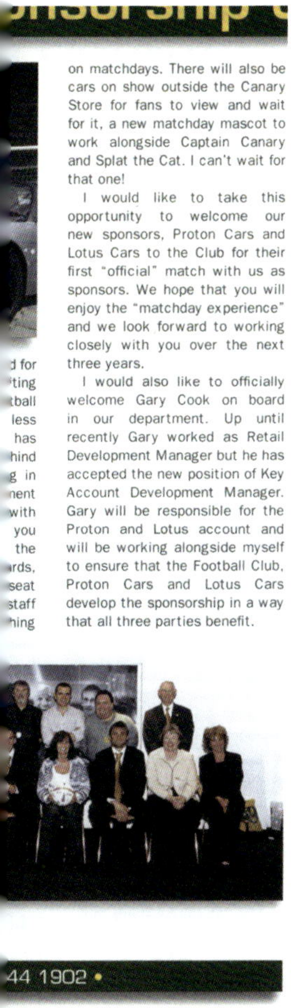
on matchdays. There will also be cars on show outside the Canary Store for fans to view and wait for it, a new matchday mascot to work alongside Captain Canary and Splat the Cat. I can't wait for that one!

I would like to take this opportunity to welcome our new sponsors, Proton Cars and Lotus Cars to the Club for their first "official" match with us as sponsors. We hope that you will enjoy the "matchday experience" and we look forward to working closely with you over the next three years.

I would also like to officially welcome Gary Cook on board in our department. Up until recently Gary worked as Retail Development Manager but he has accepted the new position of Key Account Development Manager. Gary will be responsible for the Proton and Lotus account and will be working alongside myself to ensure that the Football Club, Proton Cars and Lotus Cars develop the sponsorship in a way that all three parties benefit.

44 1902 •

Burnley

Brian Jensen, Mo Camara, Graham Branch, David May, Lee Roche, Paul Weller (Luke Chadwick), Neil Wood (Richard Chaplow), Tony Grant (Alan Moore), Glen Little, Ian Moore, Robbie Blake. Manager: Stan Ternent.

Norwich City

Robert Green, Marc Edworthy, Craig Fleming, Malky Mackay, Adam Drury, Paul McVeigh (Kevin Cooper), Gary Holt, Damien Francis, Darren Huckerby, Leon McKenzie (Philip Mulryne), Mathias Svensson (Iwan Roberts). Manager: Nigel Worthington.

Goals

Burnley: Wood (7), May (30), Blake (38)
Norwich City: Svensson (14, 62), Huckerby (32, 89), McKenzie (51)

In 2003/04 Malaysian-based Proton Cars, together with their Norfolk-based sports car manufacturing subsidiary, Lotus, agreed a three-year sponsorship deal with Norwich City. The Proton Cars' logo was carried on the club's home shirts whilst the Lotus brand was on the away shirts. Both brand logos were used on City's training kit and around the Carrow Road ground. The cars were placed on show outside the Canary Store for fans to view. The sponsorship was deemed a success by both parties, with Norwich City winning the 'Best Club Sponsorship' award in the inaugural Football League Awards in 2006. The racing green away shirt proved particularly popular in the new season as Norwich roared their way up the table.

Nigel Worthington had managed to keep the core of the squad which had been so close to winning promotion at the Millennium Stadium in 2002. But whilst he had not been able to recruit a top striker to support Iwan Roberts in the summer close season – Damien Francis had been brought in to strengthen the midfield and Marc Edworthy also arrived from Wolves in the summer – Worthington pulled off a major coup in September by recruiting Peter Crouch (Aston Villa),

25 Edward Couzens-Lake includes the Burnley vs Norwich City game of 3 April 2004 in *Greatest Games: Norwich City* (Pitch Publishing, 2012).

Darren Huckerby (Manchester City) and Kevin Harper (Portsmouth) on loan. As Roberts recalled later, the recruitment lifted both the players and the fans.[26] On 13 September all three made their debut in the home fixture against Burnley, with Crouch and Roberts scoring to give City a 2–0 win. Both Crouch and Harper returned to their clubs at the beginning of the winter, but nevertheless, when Aston Villa recalled Crouch, the Canaries were third in the table.

With Christmas approaching, Norwich signed Leon McKenzie and Mathias Svensson. Things were getting serious. By Boxing Day in December 2003, for the Canaries' fixture against Nottingham Forest, the mood was buoyant. Norwich were fresh from an away victory at Ipswich Town's Portman Road on 20 December (courtesy of a McKenzie double) and were top of the league. There was still time for chairman Roger Munby to note in the match programme that the club had worked hard to replace the lost income from the collapse of ITV Digital: £2.4 million of new cash had been raised, including enabling fans to buy a new share issue. No doubt Munby's message was timed to reassure fans as they received their best Christmas present, with Darren Huckerby appearing on the pitch along with Delia Smith and Michael Wynn-Jones before kick-off to announce his permanent signing by the club. This was pure theatre. I remember shouting loudly somewhere on a snow-covered train in Switzerland as I was treating my family to a Christmas break! This signing was certainly a powerful statement to support a renewed push to reclaim Norwich City's place in the Premier League. As Iwan Roberts said, quoted in Peter Rogers' excellent summary of the promotion-winning season, 'We might have finished in the top six and made the play-offs – we had a good side and a good spine and players with plenty of experience. But when Hucks walked through the door we knew we had a proper good chance.'[27]

Burnley welcomed Norwich City to Turf Moor on 3 April 2004. The Burnley chairman Barry Kilby noted in the match programme how important television money was to his club, and how little they were receiving. Burnley were having a poor season, and this was reflected in the television coverage they had received. First Division clubs were paid £10,000 for live away games and £60,000 for live home games

Player cards (Topps)

Author's collection

26 Roberts, 'Not the worst, after all'.

27 Peter Rogers, *Promotion-Winning Canaries: The Memories, Players, Facts and Figures Behind All Ten Norwich City Post-War Promotions* (Pitch Publishing, 2019), p. 66.

on Sky. Having only been televised once in an away match close to the beginning of the season, Burnley's total broadcasting income amounted to £10,000.

Going to away matches feels very different for football fans. Planning the trip requires considerable organisation, from managing to get a ticket in the first place, to deciding how to get to the stadium in question. In my time as a Norwich supporter, since I moved away from the fine city, I've lived in Birmingham, in the north-west of England, and in Glasgow. Believe me, I know the motorway systems and train routes in detail. Norwich City as a club have always made an effort to communicate with their away support and thus the match at Burnley featured a chance for some members of the board to meet the Northern Canaries Fan Group in a pub before the game. As ever, everyone wanted to speak to Delia Smith and, as ever, she was very willing not only to chat but also to pose for the inevitable pictures.

So we were all in a good mood with high expectations even before the match kicked off. After eight seasons out of the Premier League, Norwich were poised on the brink of return. Their side was bristling with attacking options, with McKenzie, Svensson, Roberts and Huckerby all offering alternatives for the manager. Burnley did feature some quality players, however, with goalkeeper Brian Jensen, centre-back David May, and Robbie Blake in the forward line.

And the match turned out to be a belter. Burnley scored first direct from a free kick, but Svensson equalised within seven minutes. Burnley again came back and led 2–1 with May sliding in a shot at the far post. This time Huckerby equalised, with a chip from an acute angle. But Burnley managed another before half-time as Robbie Blake made it 3–2 to the home side. However, there was no stopping Norwich City in the second half. Goals from McKenzie, Huckerby and Svensson took the Canaries to a famous 5–3 win – indeed, their first ever win at Turf Moor. Norwich City were on the way to the Premier League. They landed the Division One title whilst losing 1–0 at Sunderland on 4 May, completing the season on 94 points, eight points clear of the Division One runners-up, West Bromwich Albion. A famous season indeed. Iwan Roberts wrote it up well in his autobiography, written with Karen Buchanan.[28]

28 Iwan Roberts with Karen Buchanan, *All I Want for Christmas...* (Vision Sports Publishing, 2004).

Home and away shirts
Norwich City wore
in their successful
2003/04 season

Author's collection

This was a memorable season for Norwich City and their fans with many commemorative items to cherish

Author's collection

Player card (Topps)

Author's collection

Player card (Canary Collectables, 2001–02)

Author's collection

The Quest for the Premier League and a Financial Chasm

The never-ending battle for those clubs like Norwich marooned in Division One (renamed the Championship in 2004/05) to achieve the giddy heights of the Premier League was made increasingly hard by the growing financial chasm between the two top divisions of English football. Economists Stephen Dobson and John Goddard describe this in great detail in their book, *The Economics of Football*, published in 2011. They show the divergence in financial strength between the Premier League and the three divisions below in the Football League since the formation of the former in 1992. Between 1994 and 1996 the Premier League received 66.4% of the total revenue coming into the four divisions of professional English men's football. But from 2006 to 2008, the Premier League's share had swelled to 76.3%. There were further inequalities in both the Premier League and the Championship immediately below. Teams recently relegated from the Premier League into the Championship receive a 'parachute payment', based on a share of the Premier League's broadcast revenues, thus giving them an advantage over other clubs seeking to clamber out the division. But there are further gaps in the Premier League itself where participation in the UEFA Champions League is richly rewarded. Manchester United, the competition winners in 2008, received £34 million from UEFA's TV income, for example.

At this time, although football's matchday crowds had been transformed to produce what John Williams called 'the emergence of the regulated, individuated, surveilled and high spending bourgeoisie football audience',[29] gate revenues had fallen dramatically in comparison to broadcast income in the Premier League. And there was also less opportunity for smaller clubs to benefit from the income received from drawing larger clubs in the cup competitions, as penalty shootouts had been substituted for possibly lucrative replayed games as a means of settling drawn cup ties.

Football finance expert Kieran Maguire notes that matchday income for Manchester United in 1992 was £11.1 million.[30] Whilst this had risen to £110.8 million in 2019, this was dwarfed by the increase in broadcast

29 John Williams, 'The "new football" in England and Sir John Hall's "new Geordie nation"', in Siegfried Gehrmann (ed.), *Football and Regional Identity in Europe* (LIT Verlag, 1997), pp. 243, 244.

30 Kieran Maguire, *The Price of Football* (Agenda, 2020).

income from £1.8 million to £242.2 million. Maguire shows how payments to broadcast Premier League live matches had increased from £38 million between 1992 and 1997 to £569 million in 2007–10. And as global audiences for English top-flight football grew, the Premier League was also able to sell international broadcasting rights. In 1992–97, these were worth £3 million. By 2007–10 their worth had increased exponentially to £569 million. Clubs in the Championship would be willing to risk a lot to attain a slice of this staggering revenue.

The Canaries Flying Low

Unfortunately, the Canaries' stay in the Barclays Premiership was short-lived. After so many years marooned in Division One, their return into the top league in 2004/05 only lasted one season. Despite having won the Division One title with some style in 2004, Nigel Worthington's men, even with the redoubtable Darren Huckerby in the side, never really looked like they would survive with the big boys, although they signed Dean Ashton for a reported record fee of £3 million from Crewe in January (Iwan Roberts' contract had not been renewed at the end of City's promotion season). That being said, after winning their last four games at home (including memorable wins against Manchester United and Newcastle United), it came down to a final match away to Fulham that would determine whether Norwich City would stay up. They just needed a win to guarantee safety, and took an estimated 6,500 fans to Craven Cottage to roar them over the line.[31] They lost 6–0! The club's single season in the Premier League had nevertheless generated over £20 million of additional income, with the club turnover declared at over £37 million in the 2005 accounts.[32]

Norwich City's first season in the newly named and sponsored Coca-Cola Championship (the sponsorship deal had begun in 2004) was ultimately disappointing (they finished ninth). You can still watch the highlights on the club's YouTube channel, with the film introduced by the chairman of that time, Roger Munby. The film shows the matches through the 2005/06 season, but Munby, in his introductory piece, chooses to highlight both the part Norwich City played in the community, and the fact that, despite relegation, the club's average crowd increased in the lower league to 24,833.[33] The sale of Ashton to West Ham for £7 million

31 Woodrow, *Norwich City Football Club*, vol. IV, 13 January 2007.

32 Ibid., vol. IV, 31 October 2005.

33 'Norwich City 2005–06 Season Review', YouTube. Available at: https://www.youtube.com/watch?v=V3mKZrGsNYw (accessed 14 May 2025).

in January 2006, however, seemed to signify the club's lack of ambition with the fans. Damien Francis had left previously in a £1.5 million (with add-ons) deal with Wigan Athletic. Robbie Earnshaw was, however, signed from West Bromwich Albion for £2.75 million (this could increase depending on specified conditions being fulfilled).

Norwich kicked off the next season with a new sponsor, low fares airline Flybe. The deal meant that Flybe were associated with four different football teams, including both Norwich and their home club, Exeter, who were in the Football Conference at this time. The airline had invested in the operations base they had opened at Norwich Airport in 2004 and the 16 routes they offered from there were promoted in the Norwich City match programme.

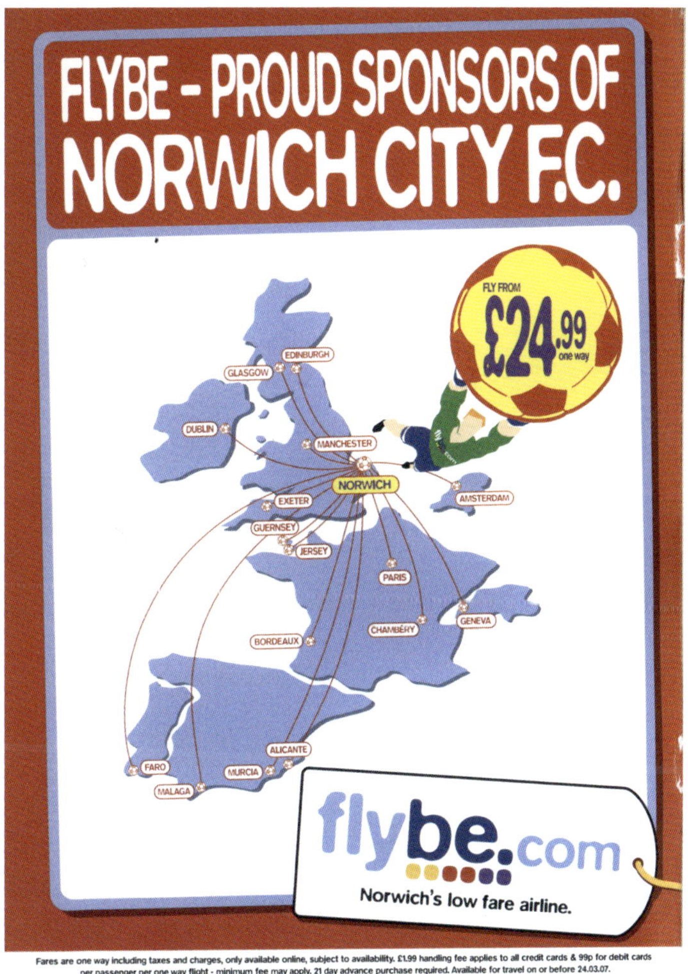

Inside front cover of match programme, Norwich City vs Sunderland, 4 November 2006

Author's collection

In March 2008 the BBC carried a story in which, bizarrely, it was reported that Flybe was advertising for actors to fly between Norwich and Dublin to try to boost passenger numbers.[34] Apparently, Norwich Airport had inserted a clause into the deal with the airline that if it didn't carry 15,000 passengers on the Dublin route, Flybe would have to pay a £280,000 penalty. It was probably not a shock when Flybe's two-year sponsorship deal with Norwich City was not renewed for the 2008/09 season.

The club's performances on the pitch seemed to mirror their sponsor's business results in the air. Both were seriously declining. Goalkeeper Robert Green was the latest big name to leave, with West Ham United paying £2 million to Norwich City in August 2006, and Leon McKenzie departed soon afterwards. Meanwhile, Dion Dublin arrived on a free transfer from Celtic in September.

City manager Nigel Worthington paid the price for the club's lowly 17th position in the Championship immediately following a 1–4 home defeat by Burnley on 1 October, when his contract was terminated. It was noted in the end-of-year accounts that Worthington's dismissal had cost Norwich City £600,000.[35] He was replaced by former player Peter Grant, who led the Canaries to a disappointing 16th place in the final Coca-Cola Football League Championship table of 2006/07. Dickson Etuhu was transferred to Sunderland for £1.5 million in July 2007, with Youssef Safri following soon afterwards to Southampton. Grant left in October 2007 following a defeat by Queens Park Rangers which left Norwich in 22nd place in the table. The new manager was Glenn Roeder. Fans will remember a 2–1 loss to League Two strugglers Bury in a third round FA Cup replay at Gigg Lane as summing up this dismal period for the club. Roeder might be best remembered for signing Wes Hoolihan from Blackpool in January 2008. It didn't help the manager though, and Roeder's stay was brief, being in post until January 2009, when Norwich's position in the Championship was under threat. Old City stalwart Bryan Gunn, now the club's head of player recruitment, was appointed manager. Performances didn't pick up, however. Norwich City's third consecutive year in the Football Championship was marked by the unthinkable. They were relegated in 22nd place and found themselves back in the third tier of English football for the first time since 1960.

34 'Airline sought actors for flights', BBC news, 30 March 2008. Available at: http://news.bbc.co.uk/1/hi/england/norfolk/7321306.stm (accessed 14 May 2025).

35 Woodrow, *Norwich City Football Club*, vol. IV, 18 June 2000.

This was a both a financial and confidence-sapping disaster. Academic John Tribe wrote a powerful piece in 2023, outlining why football clubs' financial problems are common in lower leagues, and how huge an impact this has on not only on the clubs but also their local communities.[36] Tribe provides a list of 34 English clubs that have entered insolvency procedures. These included the likes of QPR, Leicester City, Ipswich Town and Derby County. Fourteen clubs – including Bury, Macclesfield Toan, Wimbledon, Scarborough, Halifax Town and Chester – have been liquidated. As the banks were bailed out during the 2007/08 financial crisis, football clubs had to find their own way through their own crises. Tribe argues that football clubs should be treated differently from other businesses. After all, a football club is very different from a high-street store. He concluded his piece, 'football clubs are a way of life, not just businesses'.

Despite the poor footballing performances, Norwich fans felt very much the same about their club. Crowd attendances at Carrow Road remained high during this dark time. The average home attendance in 2006/07 was 24,544 and 24,527 in 2007/08, the year of their relegation.

Loyal Supporters

What defines a loyal supporter is much argued and debated both in public houses and at football grounds. What is certain though is that the relationship between fans and their clubs has been transformed since the birth of the Premier League. Whilst clubs like Norwich City continue to discuss their fans as members of their community and go to great efforts to support local causes, it is also true to say that twenty-first-century supporters have been transformed into a community of consumers.

Many of those who might consider themselves true supporters never attend matches in person but buy replica kits and other merchandise to show their favour. Since the broadcasting of regular live football, it could be argued that the pub is the modern focus of British fandom, where fans can gather together to watch a match.

There are many fan groups located both around the UK and internationally where fans can use social media to connect, and, on occasions, travel together to matches or social functions. The Norwich City board have

36 John Tribe, 'Football club collapses in lower leagues: how to avoid them for the good of the community', *The Conversation*, 20 January 2023. Available at: https://theconversation.com/football-club-collapses-in-lower-leagues-how-to-avoid-them-for-the-good-of-the-community-198244 (accessed 14 May 2025).

Northern Canaries are one of Norwich City's fan groups
Author's collection

an excellent history of meeting with supporters on such occasions to discuss everything from the price of match tickets to the strength of the current match squad. In *On the Ball*, the matchday programme produced for the Norwich vs Sunderland match on 4 November 2006, the Canaries' director of sales and marketing, Andrew Cullen, described how the club sought to engage with its supporters through its Supporters' Consultative Group (which was originally established in 1996). For example, a pre-match meeting before the fixture with Stoke City in October 2006 included representatives from Capital Canaries, Northern Canaries and Midland Canaries. Cullen also wrote about an 'Image and Identity Working Party' which was looking at 'how the Norwich City brand might evolve'. This is probably not the kind of language that is likely to engage the typical fan!

Joe Ferrari, now media manager of Norwich City, wrote at the start of the 2008/09 season about the impact of the 'internet revolution' in his piece in the Norwich vs Blackpool match programme. The Norwich match against Spurs (a pre-season friendly) on 28 July had been live-streamed for the first time to CanariesWorld subscribers on the club website. And the internet was certainly influencing how fans engaged with their team. At the same time, although Ferrari doesn't address this, it was influencing how fans were being persuaded to consume more. And not only replica shirts.

Many football fans do choose to reject perceived consumerism. The rejection of consumerism was at least one of the reasons behind the actions of one group of Manchester United supporters in establishing FC United of Manchester in 2005, following the takeover of the club by the Glazer family, in a sign of opposition to the 'development of the club as a global leisure brand'.[37] FC United was seen as a counterpoint to corporate, consumer-driven football culture and incorporated an opposition to 'plastic' (inauthentic) fans.

37 Adam Brown, '"Our club, our rules": fan communities at FC United of Manchester', *Soccer and Society*, 9.3 (2008), p. 347.

northern canaries

northern canaries
Northern Forum 2005
11 February 2005 - Kick Off 7:00pm
Ruskin Hotel
Albert Road
Blackpool
www.northerncanaries.com • persistent standing is not allowed

Match Report: Saturday 8 August 2009, k/o 15:00.
Coca-Cola League One, Carrow Road,
Norwich City 1 Colchester United 7. Attendance: 25,217

Norwich City
Michael Theoklitos, Jon Otsemobor, Michael Nelson, Gary Doherty, Adam Drury, Simon Whaley, Matthew Gill (Tom Adeyemi), Owain Tudur-Jones, Wes Hoolihan, Grant Holt, Chris Martin (Cody McDonald). Manager: Bryan Gunn.

Colchester United
Ben Williams, Lee Beevers, Magnus Okuonghae, Pat Baldwin, Marc Tierney, Dean Hammond, David Fox, Simon Hackney (David Perkins), Ashley Vincent (Kemal Izzet), Clive Platt, Kevin Lisbie (Scott Vernon). Manager: Paul Lambert.

Goals
Norwich City: McDonald (72)
Colchester United: Lisbie (10, 38), Platt (13, 19), Fox (22), Perkins (76), Vernon (90)

Norwich City's first opponents in Coca-Cola League One in August 2009 were Colchester United. This was a cold introduction to the football world below the Championship. It was the first time Norwich City had been at this level for fifty years. And it hurt. It was a season when the Canaries would be travelling to much smaller venues than Carrow Road, where the money was even tighter. The Essex club were visiting from their new Weston Homes Community Stadium, which had a capacity of 10,000. They had moved from their former ground at Layer Road, just a season previously, following considerable help from Colchester Borough Council in raising the £14 million needed to build the new stadium. United were managed by former Celtic and Scotland international Paul Lambert, whilst former Norwich player Gary Holt was in the Colchester squad.

Relegation had been a huge shock to the system and had involved a huge intake and exodus of players. Experienced professionals such as goalkeeper David Marshall and midfielders Lee Croft and Sammy Clingan bailed out to clubs higher up the league ladder. The newcomers included Grant Holt, a striker bought from Shrewsbury Town for £500,000, and Michael Nelson, a defender from Hartlepool. Both of these players would have big parts to play in the season to come. Wes Hoolihan, a future legend for the club, also featured in the opening-day fixture.

Front cover of match programme, Norwich City vs Colchester United, 8th August 2009, featuring Simon Whaley

Author's collection

One of eleven new signings, he got off to a great start in our 7-1 defeat, four games later he went out on loan

Matt Gill had been brought in by Bryan Gunn on a free from Exeter City in the pre-season period. Gill had previous ties with Norfolk and there is a nice interview with him in the Colchester match programme. As he explained, 'First games of the season are always massive occasions whoever you are playing and especially when you are at home.' He continued, 'We need to get off to a good start. Momentum is a massive thing in football and if we can get that momentum flowing in the right way who knows where it can take us.' I have no idea how Matt felt after that match with Colchester, but I am fairly clear how I and the other 25,000 odd Canaries fans felt!

Bryan Gunn's first league match as Norwich City manager in the 2009/10 season was also his last. Grant Holt describes the match against Colchester in his autobiography.[38] *Norwich's new goalkeeper, Michael Theoklitos, has gone down in Canaries' folklore for his performance. And not in a good way. As Holt tells it, by 22 minutes Norwich were 0–4 down with at least three goals considered to be goalkeeping errors. At this point, two City fans had run on to the pitch towards the dugout and thrown their season tickets on the ground in disgust. A bit ironic, as Gunn had thanked the club's 18,800 season ticket holders in the match programme. Their help, and a financial assist by club director Michael Foulger, had helped bring Holt to the club from Shrewsbury Town. City were 0–5 down at half-time. I remember texting the score to a pal who simply didn't believe me. I'm not sure I quite believed myself.*

The match eventually finished 1–7, the worst home defeat in Norwich's 107-year history. It was the first time they had lost by such a score since their drubbing by Blackburn Rovers in the first season of the Premier League back in 1992, another game that I had been unfortunate enough to watch. As a match commentator at the Colchester game wisely said about Bryan Gunn, 'Being a club legend counts for nothing when your side is being ripped to shreds.' Holt recalls 'huge boos' from the fans at the end.[39] *To be honest I was so stunned that I don't think I really said anything.*

Meantime, Joe Ferrari, writing from the comparative safety of the press box, noted that the club's relegation in May had indicated that Norwich City were ready for new ideas after the chief executive (Neil

38 Grant Holt with Daniel Brigham, *A Real Football Life: Grant Holt, My Autobiography* (twocan, 2019).

39 Ibid., p. 155.

Doncaster) and chairman (Roger Munby) had both resigned in the summer. David McNally, the new chief executive, had been Celtic's director of sales and marketing and managing director of Fulham. This was arguably a bigger signing than Holt. McNally was focused immediately on the business side of the club. Gunn's dismissal on 14 August after the club had won a cup game 4–0 against Yeovil just three days after the Colchester debacle showed that Norwich's new chief executive meant business.

McNally reinforced his determination to change things by announcing the appointment of Paul Lambert as Norwich City's new manager on 18 August. Lambert had jumped ship from Colchester. In the football world, it's often a matter of dog eats dog.

Rising Again

The 2008/09 season had certainly started promisingly with the announcement of Aviva as Norwich City's new shirt sponsor in April, after Flybe had revealed they would not be renewing their deal. It was the beginning of a twelve-year partnership in which Aviva acted both as main club sponsor and community partner. Aviva's sponsorship announcement was timed to coincide with the scrapping of the Norwich Union brand and to signify the insurance giant's commitment to the city where it still employed 6,700 people. Aviva was also the sponsor of UK athletics at this time. The sponsor gave out 5,000 special edition flags and 5,000 'bam bam' sticks to supporters prior to the match against Colchester at Carrow Road. They hoped to create a buzz ... but not perhaps the noise heard from the fans after the result.

The appointments of David McNally and Paul Lambert in 2009 marked a new steely determination to help the Canaries fly again, and ensure that they would only have a one-season stay in League One. The financial injections given to their clubs by the new owners of Chelsea and Manchester City, however, showed what clubs such as Norwich would be up against in the new decade.

AVIVA
errea

THE 2010s AND BEYOND

Money Changes Every-thing

Money Changes Everything

2010 General Election held in May results in a coalition government between the Conservatives and the Liberal Democrats with David Cameron as Prime Minister; UEFA establishes its Club Licensing and Financial Fair Play Regulations

2011 American billionaire Stan Kroenke takes a controlling interest in Arsenal FC

2012 The London Summer Olympics

2014 Scotland votes to remain in the UK after an independence referendum

2015 David Cameron and the Conservatives win the General Election

2016 The 'Big Five' clubs (Arsenal, Chelsea, Liverpool, Manchester City and Manchester United) meet to discuss forming a breakaway Super League with other European elite teams; Brexit – the withdrawal of the United Kingdom from the European Union following a referendum held on 23 June; Brexit is finally 'delivered' on 31 January 2020; David Cameron resigns as Prime Minister and Theresa May replaces him; West Ham United move into the former 2012 Olympic Stadium

2016–19 The live rights to broadcast the Premier League in the UK are awarded to Sky/BT Sport for £5.14 billion

2019 Theresa May resigns as Prime Minister and is replaced by Boris Johnson; Tottenham Hotspur move into their purpose-built stadium; Conservative Party under Boris Johnson win the General Election in December

2020 The coronavirus pandemic; the Premier League suspends its 2019/20 season on 13 March; matches resume on 17 June 2020 with the football season ending on 12 September 2020. Spectators are generally unable to attend football matches in the UK for much of the 2019/20 season and all of the 2020/21 season; Wrexham AFC is sold to RR McReynolds Company LLC; Bury FC expelled from the Football League after financial difficulties

2021 Euro 2020, postponed because of COVID-19, takes place in June and July 2021; Proposed European Super League; Newcastle United FC are taken over by a consortium including the sovereign wealth fund of Saudia Arabia

previous spread: Aviva (formerly Norwich Union) was the main sponsor of Norwich City from 2008 to 2017. Background: Ticket from the Championship play-off final, 25 May 2015.

Author's collections

Uncertainty and the Triumphs of the Billionaires

The UK election result of May 2010 heralded a decade of uncertainty and turmoil which concluded with the first worldwide public health pandemic since the influenza disaster which followed the First World War. At the same time, whilst governments preached austerity, people had less and less money in their pockets, and we saw the explosion of food banks as an emergency measure across the country. The London Olympics in the summer of 2012 were a triumph as a spectacle but hid the divisions widening across British society. Following Manchester City's move into the Commonwealth Games stadium, West Ham United were able to benefit from taxpayers' money in acquiring the London Olympic Stadium as the club's new home in 2016.

However, there were still profits to be had and speculators made large sums from gambling that the UK would vote to leave the European Union in June 2016. In English football, American billionaire businessmen were gradually making their mark and continuing the process of transforming the game. None more so than Stan Kroenke, the owner of Kroenke Sports & Entertainment, who took a controlling interest in Arsenal in April 2011.

The increasingly huge amounts that broadcasters were willing to pay to gain exclusive rights to show the English Premier League enabled Sky to establish itself as 'the leading sports and entertainment platform in the UK'.[1] The Premier League also gained a global audience, which encouraged advertisers and sponsors to pour money into the game: their brands were often aimed at consumers on the other side of the world, and match kick-off times reflected this.

And whilst West Ham United and Tottenham Hotspur moved into their shiny new stadiums, their business plans were focused on increasing the corporate spend. More and more supporters became increasingly vocal that ticket prices and game times were excluding them from their club. The game was changing, turning into something the fans were not sure they wanted to be a part of.[2]

So, in some ways it was timely when the coronavirus pandemic brought global economies to a juddering halt during the 2020/21 football season. Fans were largely excluded from stadiums because of public health

1 Daniel Geey, *Done Deal: An Insider's Guide to Football Contracts, Multi-Million Pound Transfers and Premier League Big Business* (Bloomsbury Sport, 2019), p. 201.

2 Brian Williams, *Home from Home: A West Ham Supporter's Struggle to Reach the Next Level* (Biteback Publishing, 2017).

concerns, and the football business, like all other aspects of society, had time to look closely into its soul to reflect on its values and ethics.

Player cards (Topps Match Attax)
Author's collection

The World's Game Played in England

In 2007 Gordon Taylor, the then chief executive of the Professional Footballers' Association (a post he held for over forty years from 1981 to 2021), argued that the presence of a large number of overseas players in the Premier League was having a negative effect on the development of home-grown players and, indeed, on the English national team.[3] Taylor noted that since the beginning of the Premier League in 1992, the percentage of English players starting matches in the top flight had shrunk by 47%. The former England manager Gareth Southgate had the same lament in 2023, except that now only about 32% of those starting matches in the highest league were eligible for England. Indeed, the figure is even lower (27%) if you consider the playing time of English players at the traditional six big clubs. In 2007 Taylor wrote that England's failure to qualify for the Euro 2008 finals was due to 'only one source: English football is running out of English players'.

The commercial strength of the English Premier League, and indeed other Western European leagues, inevitably attracts players from across the world seeking to improve their living and working conditions.[4] The migration of African and Latin American players to more lucrative leagues can, in contrast, leave their own leagues underdeveloped. Players are lured by the promise of higher salaries and exposure in Europe's glamorous and prestigious football competitions. Richard Elliott argues that these migrations are a signifier of the process of globalisation.[5] And, of course, it develops the spectacle of the Premier League as a global entertainment product featuring some of the world's best players.

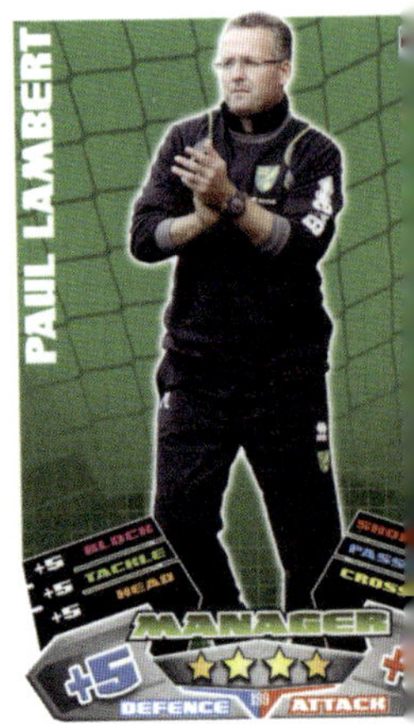

Back to the Glory Days

Norwich had started the new decade in the best way possible. Paul Lambert's team had done him proud, and back-to-back promotions followed as they stormed back from the Coca-Cola Football League One to the Barclays Premier League, barely pausing for breath in their single season in the Npower Championship. City finished nine points ahead of

3 Gordon Taylor, 'Meltdown: the nationality of Premier League players and the future of English football', *Birkbeck Sport Business Centre Research Paper Series* 2, no. 2 (2009), pp. 51–70.

4 Richard Elliott, 'Chasing the ball', in Richard Elliott and John Harris (eds), *Football and Migration: Perspectives, Places, Players* (Routledge, 2015).

5 Ibid.

Leeds United as League One champions in 2009/10. Amidst a number of players brought in by Lambert to strengthen a promotion challenge, Russell Martin joined City from Peterborough United in January 2010 (he had originally arrived on loan). Stephen Fry even joined the party in August 2010, becoming one of the club's directors. The season in the Championship certainly brought some highlights for City fans with a high-scoring double over Ipswich Town (the 4–1 win at Carrow Road in November included a Grant Holt hat-trick). Promotion was secured with a memorable Simeon Jackson goal at Portsmouth in May 2011. Norwich City were runners-up to the champions, Queens Park Rangers.

After being promoted back to the Premier League, Lambert even secured a 12th place finish for Norwich in 2011/12 and with no big-name signings, although there were incomers including Bradley Johnson, Anthony Pilkington and Daniel Ayala (the latter for £750,000 from Liverpool). Jonny Howson joined from Leeds United in January 2012. The financial benefits of a return to the top level of English football were immediately clear. It was announced at the beginning of the season that all Premier League clubs would receive £13.8 million a season from the sale of domestic television rights and a further £17.9 million from overseas rights. Additional income would be received based on final league position and the number of times a club's matches were broadcast live on TV.[6]

But as with players, so with managers. If the big clubs come calling and the money is right, departure soon follows. To the chagrin of Norwich fans, Lambert followed the script, leaving for Aston Villa in June 2012. Chris Hughton was the replacement, a no-nonsense Londoner who had had previous success with Newcastle United, and, to a lesser extent, with Birmingham City. Signings at the beginning of the 2012/13 season included Sébastien Bassong from Tottenham Hotspur and Alexander Tettey from Stade Rennais. One Harry Kane also joined City on loan from Tottenham Hotspur (he was recalled by Spurs in January 2013 after a generally unsuccessful stay). Hughton's main priority was simply to keep Norwich in the Premier League, and, to that extent, he was successful at least for one season; Norwich finished 11th on his watch. But the football was patchy and unexciting, and the club even managed to lose 1–0 at home to non-league Luton Town in the fourth round of the FA Cup (the first time a Premier League club had lost to a non-league club in the competition).

6 James Woodrow (as compiled for the Norwich City Football Club), *Norwich City Football Club: The Archive* (Severn, 2022), vol. IV, 21 August 2011.

One high point in the season was Norwich City's triumph in the FA Youth Cup, winning a two-leg final 4–2 in April and May 2013 against Chelsea. This was a tremendous achievement for the underdogs. Liverpool, Manchester City, Arsenal, Chelsea (twice) and Manchester United had been the previous winners, and Chelsea went on to win the Youth Cup for the five seasons after Norwich's victory.

Despite this success, it is a sign of the times that only three of the Canaries' 2012/13 Youth Cup squad have gone on to play in the Premier League. Jacob Murphy has been the most successful, still playing an active role in the Newcastle United squad in 2024/25. Harry Toffolo and Carlton Morris have also played in the top division with Nottingham Forest and Luton Town respectively. Jacob Murphy's twin, Josh, was playing for Championship club Portsmouth in the 2024/25 season.

Norwich managed three consecutive seasons in the Premier League between 2011 and 2014. Despite the departure of talisman Grant Holt, the 2012/13 season started promisingly with seven new signings, including Swedish international Martin Olsson, Dutchman Leroy Fer, Nathan Redmond, Steven Whittaker and Gary Hooper (for £5.2 million from Celtic). It was Ricky van Wolfswinkel who caught the headlines, however. Van Wolkswinkel arrived for a reported record fee of £8.5 million from Sporting Lisbon in 2013 (more than was reproduced on the accompanying player card) in the club's latest effort to make their mark in the Premier League. The fans liked Ricky. He looked like the star striker Norwich City needed. Indeed, the Canaries' marketing slogan in August 2013 was 'Beware the Wolf'. Sadly for the Norfolk team, van Wolfswinkel only scored one league goal for Norwich in his three years with the club, and that was in their opening game of his first season.

Player cards (Topps Match Attax) Ricky van Wolkswinkel and Chris Hughton. Neither proved good 'fits' for Norwich City

Author's collection

The fate of the marquee signing probably summed up Norwich City's season. They spent much of the season in the lower half of the league, but poor performances in the last few matches led to relegation and a return to the Sky Bet Championship. Chris Hughton was sacked in April 2014 with just five matches to go and was replaced by Neil Adams, who had coached the Youth Cup winning team.

Joe Ferrari, still head of media at Norwich City in 2013, reflected on the pulling power of the Premier League in his piece in the match programme for the opening home game of the 2013/14 season. The league claimed that 804 million homes in 212 countries around the world received Premier League football. This huge audience brought in substantial income for all the Premier League clubs based on 'an influx of increased interest and investment from new and existing foreign and domestic media rightsholders'.[7] Norwich City were desperate to find a way back to this competition of footballing riches.

Match Report: Saturday 19 January 2013, k/o 15:00.
Barclays Premier League, Anfield, Liverpool 5 Norwich 0.
Attendance: 44,901.

Liverpool
Brad Jones, Lucas Leiva (Raheem Sterling), Glen Johnson, Jamie Carragher, Andre Wisdom, Stewart Downing, Daniel Agger, Jordan Henderson (Joe Allen), Daniel Sturridge (Fabio Borini), Luis Suárez, Steven Gerrard. Manager: Brendan Rodgers.

Norwich City
Mark Bunn, Alexander Tettey, Javier Garrido, Michael Turner, Russell Martin, Bradley Johnson, Robert Snodgrass (Anthony Pilkington), Grant Holt, Ryan Bennett, Elliott Bennett (Wes Hoolihan), Jonathan Howson. Manager: Chris Hughton.

Goals
Liverpool: Henderson (26), Suárez (36), Sturridge (59), Gerrard (66), R. Bennett (o.g., 74)

It is always a tough call for a club like Norwich City to visit Anfield. The task had become greater given the resources and players available to Liverpool, who had been ever present in the Premier League and whose expectations each season were to achieve European success in addition to domestic league and cup triumphs. Liverpool's sponsors in 2012/13 – see the image taken from the match programme below – reflected the global brand that Liverpool had become. Standard Chartered – a global financial services company – took over from Carlsberg as Liverpool FC's shirt sponsor in 2010 and has remained so ever since. The original deal was reportedly worth £20 million a year[8] – a figure which has risen considerably since then. One of Liverpool's sponsors that same season was Thomas Cook, as reflected in the

7 Joe Ferrari, 'Pressing Matters', in *On the Ball City*, official matchday programme for Norwich City vs Everton, Barclays Premier League, 17 August 2013.

8 Rory Jones, 'Liverpool score "UK£50m a year" Standard Chartered extension', *SportsPro*, 14 July 2022. Available at: https://www.sportspromedia.com/news/liverpool-standard-chartered-shirt-sponsorship-extension-premier-league/ (accessed 24 September 2024).

Official Liverpool FC Match Breaks being offered to fans.[9] *That's what you get when you have a global brand: people coming from all over the world to watch 'your' club. No doubt some of these tourists chose to purchase a 'half-and-half' scarf, but 'traditional' fans hate this.*[10] *To them, it's proof that football culture has changed for the worse. The game has always been about wearing your colours, not someone else's. But the 'half-and-half' scarf firmly marks a match as the entertainment product it has become. It is just another piece of 'merch' to say you were there.*

Liverpool's team on 19 January 2013 was full of internationals, including England players Jamie Carragher, Glen Johnson, Stewart Downing, Jordan Henderson, Steven Gerrard and Daniel Sturridge. But Uruguayan international Luis Suárez was perhaps the biggest name on the field. Suárez had originally come to Ajax in Amsterdam from Montevideo, but was then recruited by Kenny Dalglish to Liverpool in 2011 for a reported €26.5 million. When Suárez moved from Merseyside to FC Barcelona in 2014, the Catalan club paid €81.7 million for him. These are huge transfer figures, especially when compared to Norwich City, whose reported record transfer fee for a player came in January 2016 when they bought Steven Naismith from Everton for around £8 million. And you get what you pay for. Naismith made 44 appearances in his three years for Norwich (2016–19), scoring six goals. In contrast, Suárez – over a similar timeframe – made 191 appearances for Liverpool, scoring 69 goals. Sadly for Norwich City, 12 of these goals were scored against them, including two hat-tricks at Carrow Road in 2012 (in the 2011/12 and 2012/13 seasons).

When the Canaries travelled to Anfield in January 2013, they were rather surprisingly only four places behind Liverpool in the Barclays Premier League – the Merseyside giants were in a lowly eighth place, 24 points behind Manchester United in Sir Alex Ferguson's final season. However, the previous five games between the clubs did not provide an encouraging sign. Of those matches (spread across eight years), Liverpool had won four, with the sole exception being a memorable 1–1 draw the previous season (October 2011) when Grant Holt secured a point with a brilliant headed equaliser. Those five games featured the reds scoring 14 goals, with the yellows responding with a paltry four.

9 Gareth Roberts, 'Half and half scarves: two-team trash that belongs in the bin', *The Anfield Wrap*, 24 March 2015. Available at: https://www.theanfieldwrap.com/2015/03/half-and-half-scarves-two-team-trash-that-belongs-in-the-bin/ (accessed 24 September 2024).

10 Ibid.

Norwich went into the game having only secured one point from their previous four league games (a goalless draw at home to Newcastle). Manager Chris Hughton is quoted in the Liverpool programme concerning the January transfer window: 'We're working hard, there's no doubt about that. You hope you can be successful but it's about making sure anything we do is right for this football club.' This is the story of the modern club. In December 2003 the Norfolk side, pushing for promotion, had announced the signing of Darren Huckerby. Just under ten years later it was all about trying to survive in the Premier League.

Liverpool, under Brendan Rodgers, had not started the season as well as they had would have hoped. They had lost 2–1 at Manchester United the previous Saturday and suffered a 3–1 defeat at Stoke City on Boxing Day. They had, however, reached the Europa League knockout stage, and were looking forward to return fixtures with Zenit St Petersburg the following month (Liverpool went on to lose over the two legs, having lost 0–2 in the opening game at Zenit's Petrovsky Stadium).

As a modern-day Norwich fan, you arrive at stadiums like Anfield hoping that your club does not let you down and that they avoid a complete shellacking. You know you're going to be patronised by the opposition, whose fans who will only ever see you as 'little Norwich', and they will of course expect an overwhelming victory. Which is, sadly for me and the visiting Norwich fans, exactly what Liverpool achieved that afternoon.

Perhaps the only positive for Norwich was that the fixture in January 2013 did not feature one of Luis Suárez's hat-tricks. In the Uruguayan's autobiography, he reflects that pretty much every shot of his seemed to land in the net when Liverpool played the Canaries: 'That would have gone in against Norwich.'[11]

And indeed, every shot from the Liverpool team did seem to go in that January afternoon. First, the ball broke kindly for Jordan Henderson who lashed a powerful shot into the top corner from just outside the penalty box. Goal number two – 12 minutes later – came from Suárez himself (cue comment on the match clips from the TV commentator: 'He loves the sight of Canary yellow'), with a neat stroke of the ball past Mark Bunn following a long pass forward and a lovely dummy from Daniel Sturridge which created the space. 2–0 to Liverpool at

11 Luis Suárez, *Crossing the Line: My Story* (Headline, 2014), p. 182.

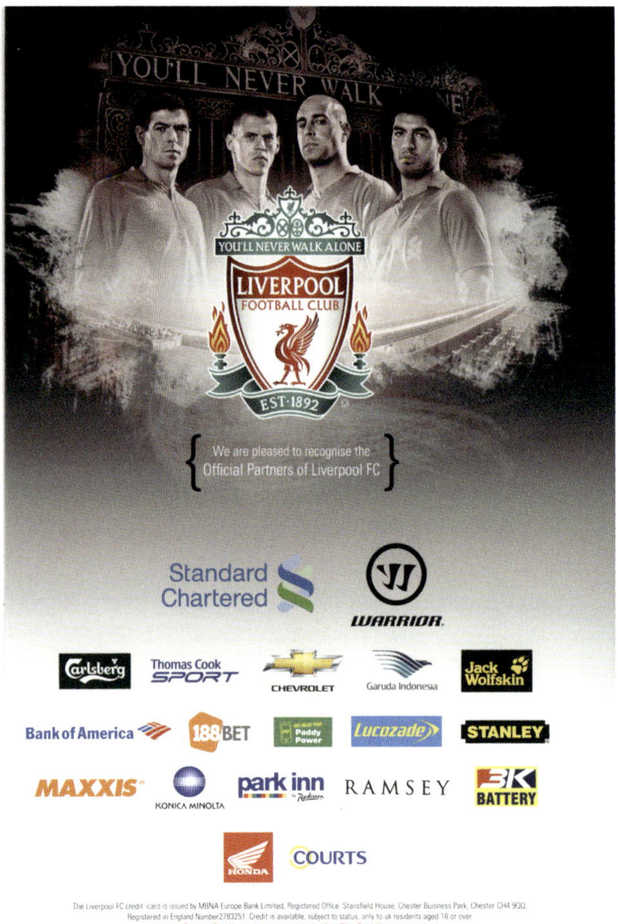

Front cover of match programme, Liverpool vs Norwich City, 19 January 2013

Liverpool FC sponsors in 2012/13. Listed in match programme

Author's collection

A 'half-and-half' scarf. One for the tourists only?

Author's collection

half-time. I feared the worst. The third goal duly arrived in the 59th minute courtesy of a easy finish for Sturridge himself from a cross from Stewart Downing. It was Steven Gerrard's turn for a long-distance strike just seven minutes later. And finally, another Norwich moment, when central defender Ryan Bennett had little choice but to divert a Raheem Sterling cross into his own net with Borini waiting to pounce behind him.

The Richest Game in Football

Richard Foster has written an excellent and entertaining history of the Football League play-offs.[12] They have certainly changed a lot since being introduced in the 1986/87 season as a means of restructuring the number of teams in the divisions. Until 1990 they were two-legged ties, and for their first two seasons the four teams involved included the top three teams in the lower division that had not achieved automatic promotion, plus the club that had finished directly above the automatic relegation places in the division above.

Given the state of football in the 1980s, as described earlier, the play-offs were introduced as one of a number of measures designed to bring the crowds back into stadiums. And they were a huge success right from the beginning, bringing excitement and anticipation for many teams, with the possibility of making a last dash to qualify when the season might otherwise have drifted to a conclusion. Once the format changed to a single tie, and the venue moved to Wembley in 1990, fans and players alike had a showpiece event to aim at. Foster argues that the play-offs have been so successful that the Championship play-off for promotion to the Premier League is now arguably as big as the FA Cup Final. And unlike the FA Cup Final, or indeed the Champions League Final, a club's fans are more than likely to be able to get a ticket for the event, whilst, for elite football's showpiece events, the majority of tickets seemed to be hoovered up by the corporate guests and football's officialdom. Indeed, Foster claims that the play-offs 'should be rightfully regarded as one of the saviours of English league football in inspiring and leading its remarkable recovery over the last few decades'.[13] He makes an excellent case, in particular by pointing out that whilst attendances in Division

12 Richard Foster, *The Agony & The Ecstasy: A Comprehensive History of the Football League Play-Offs* (Ockley Books, 2015).

13 Ibid., p. xxiii.

One fell between 1986 and 1990, they actually rose across Divisions Two, Three and Four.

And there is of course a connection with American sport, as with many other recent innovations to our traditional game, although the first link is historical. William McGregor, the founder of the Football League in 1888, drew on the play-off system used in American baseball and other sports to provide movement between the two original divisions formed in English football at the beginning of the twentieth century. However, as Foster describes, the changes introduced to the Football League in 1986 were based firmly on the American model of a series of knockout matches taking place after the season has ended to determine the overall champions. In England, though, they are all about promotion from lower leagues. And thus, they are even more valuable to the eventual play-off winners.

Foster provides a handy table demonstrating the value of the Championship play-offs. In 1987 they were worth £500,000 to Charlton Athletic, who beat Leeds United 2–1 in a replay staged at St Andrew's Stadium, Birmingham. In 2003, the year after Norwich lost to Birmingham City at the Millennium Stadium, Wolves defeated Sheffield United 3–0 at the same venue, with the match estimated as being worth £40 million. In 2013 when Crystal Palace secured victory over Watford after extra time, the value of the win had soared even higher to be estimated at £120 million. This is based on the value of finishing bottom of the Premier League and parachute payments after relegation. Parachute payments had been introduced in 2006 to alleviate the financial risk, mainly accrued from high player wages, involved in dropping down a division. Of course, the finances are more complicated than this, but the huge revenues accessed by being a member of the Premier League tempt clubs into even bigger risks to try to secure their place at the table.

However you cut the cake, the Championship play-off final is the richest game in football

Match Report: Monday 25 May 2015, k/o 15:00.
Sky Bet Championship Play-Off Final, Wembley,
Middlesbrough 0 Norwich 2. Attendance: 85,656.

Middlesbrough
Dimitrios Konstantopoulos, Dean Whitehead (Emilio Nsue), Daniel Ayala, Ben Gibson, George Friend, Adam Clayton, Grant Leadbitter, Albert Adoma, Jelle Vossen ('Kike' García Martinez), Lee Tomlin, Patrick Bamford. Head Coach: Aitor Karanka.

Norwich City
John Ruddy, Steven Whittaker, Russell Martin, Sebastien Bassong, Martin Olsson, Nathan Redmond (Gary O'Neil), Jonny Howson, Alexander Tettey, Bradley Johnson, Wes Hoolihan (Graham Dorrans), Cameron Jerome (Lewis Grabban). Manager: Alex Neil.

Goals
Norwich City: Jerome (12), Redmond (15)

Following their relegation to the Sky Bet Championship in 2014, Norwich City started the new season with Neil Adams in charge. Robert Snodgrass left for Hull in June for an estimated fee of over £7 million, City's record transfer fee for a player. Others followed, with Cameron Jerome arriving from Stoke City. In the New Year, following a series of inconsistent performances, Adams resigned. The Canaries had won at Ipswich at the start of the season, and as recently as December had enjoyed big wins at Carrow Road over Huddersfield Town (5–0) and Millwall (6–1). However, their away form was much patchier with Middlesbrough having thrashed them 4–0 in November, and Norwich had only won one game on the road in the previous six and lost 0–2 to Preston North End in the FA Cup third round on 3 January (having already been defeated by League Two Shrewsbury Town in the League Cup in September). Having enjoyed three consecutive seasons in the Premier League, David McNally and the Norwich City board would have been anxious to get back there as soon as possible.

On 9 January 2015 Adams was replaced by little-known Scotsman Alex Neil, from Hamilton Academicals. Although Neil had enjoyed considerable success at Hamilton, albeit over a short period, this seemed a leap of faith by McNally, with Neil being only 33 years old at the time of his appointment. When Norwich played at Eddie Howe's Bournemouth the following day on 10 January, Neil stayed in the stands for the majority of the match, having left the team preparation

Player cards (Topps Match Attax)
Author's collection

to Mike Phelan and Gary Holt who were in temporary charge that week. The new manager's presence seemed to have an immediate effect though. Norwich went 1–0 down to the league leaders after 18 minutes but, not long before half-time, Gary Hooper got an equaliser. Even though Jonny Howson was sent off in the second half, Cameron Jerome grabbed the winner with just ten minutes left on the clock.

When Norwich played Cardiff City one week later they were in seventh place, just eight points behind the clubs in the automatic promotion places (Bournemouth and Derby County) and only a single point behind the final play-off position. Captain Russell Martin, writing in the Cardiff match programme, said he felt that finishing in the top two places was still a possibility: 'I'd gamble on automatic.'

Norwich City didn't manage that, but nevertheless Neil's appointment turned out to be an inspired decision. Norwich gained 17 wins from 25 games under the new manager and qualified for the Championship play-offs in some style, finishing the season in third place, just three points behind Bournemouth and Watford and automatic promotion. Meanwhile Middlesbrough had finished one place and one point behind Norwich in fourth, but they had done the double over the Norfolk side during the league season. The thumping they had given the Canaries in November at the Riverside had been followed by a 1–0 win at Carrow Road on 17 April, only just over a month previously.

Before describing the final, it would be remiss not to mention the two-legged play-off semi-final between Norwich City and Ipswich Town – 'one of the biggest East Anglian showdowns in the history of the Old Farm derby'.[14] In truth though, the Norfolk club cruised past this ominous-looking stumbling block relatively comfortably. The match ended 1–1 at Portman Road, and, in the second leg at Carrow Road, Norwich won 3–1 with goals from Hoolahan, Redmond and Jerome, after Ipswich defender Berra had been sent off for handling a goal-bound shot on the line. Norwich City were back at Wembley for the first time since their Milk Cup victory over Sunderland in 1985.

Surprisingly for a club that has yo-yoed between the Championship and the Premier League, this was only Norwich's second play-off final. For me and many other younger fans (given it was thirty years since that Milk Cup victory), this was our first trip to Wembley. And

14 Rhys Griffiths, 'A League of its Own', *Sky Bet Championship Play-Off Final Official Matchday Programme*, 25 May 2015.

Match programme and ticket from the Championship play-off final, 25 May 2015

Author's collection

Player card
(Topps Match Attax)
Author's collection

like pretty much every single Norwich fan, I was as excited about the coming match as I had been for any previous fixture. I travelled to Wembley on a coach organised by the Northern Canaries fan group, which felt just right – we'd generally only been able to meet up at matches or for a quick pint before a game, so this was quite special.

Peter Rogers interviewed Russell Martin for his memories of the match and the build-up to it.[15] *Oddly, I felt a little like the captain: 'It was such a relaxed week or ten days leading to the final. You just had that feeling it was going to go for us.' Whilst the new Wembley was a bit of a disappointment with its corporate fast-food franchises, nothing else let us down. As a Norwich fan, being part of a sea of yellow and green feels like nothing else.*

And Norwich City, in the second play-off final of their history, came out convincing winners. After just nine minutes Bradley Johnson had clattered a shot against the crossbar, to be immediately followed by a similar effort from Jelle Vossen with a similar result. But that was possibly the Teesside team's one and only chance of victory. Just a few minutes later, Cameron Jerome robbed a dawdling Daniel Ayala, and made a tricky finish seem simple as he slotted in at the near post. Technically, as the TV commentator said, this was Norwich's first ever goal at Wembley, as their goal against Sunderland in 1985 has gone down as an own goal. And just a few minutes later, still within the first 15 minutes, the Canaries stole the ball again – this time in midfield – and one good pass later from Steven Whittaker, it was Nathan Redmond finishing with aplomb with a low shot from just inside the right of the penalty box. 'A blistering start from Norwich City', said the TV commentator, and indeed it was. There was no way back for Boro. Back to Russell Martin again to sum up the day: 'That was the ultimate for me – leading the team up the steps at Wembley, and to do it in front of all those fans and your family was brilliant. It was magical and something you can only dream of really. That was the highlight of my career.'[16] *It was a day I will certainly never forget.*

The task for Alex Neil and his men was, once again – now they were back in the Premier League – to see whether they could stay there. And, as the play-off final took place after the 2014/15 season's fixtures had ended on 2 May, Norwich City were already three weeks behind Bournemouth and Watford, who had secured their promotion places then.

15 Pete Rogers, *Promotion-Winning Canaries: The Memories, Players, Facts and Figures Behind All Ten Norwich City Post-War Promotions* (Pitch Publishing, 2019), p. 95.

16 Ibid.

The Replica Shirt Game

The replica kit market has become big business and another source of income for clubs. Kit launches with beautifully crafted short films featuring male and female players are now expected, and indeed looked forward to, by fans before the kick-off of a new season. Indeed, there may even be kit launches for away strips and third kits.

The story of the development of the replica kit industry is told by academics and shirt enthusiasts alike.[17] Many clubs' fans, including those of Norwich City,[18] lovingly document the history of their clubs' shirts (as well as building large collections of them). Like all other aspects of the game, football shirts have been customised to make the greatest amount of profit for both the shirt manufacturers and the football clubs, with, unusually and arguably, the willing acquiescence of the fans themselves.

Admiral can claim to be the company that changed replica football shirts from children's sportswear to adult leisurewear. Admiral used the 1968 Copyright Act to achieve exclusivity for what was originally children's replica kit. But they realised very swiftly that there was also a market for adults to wear copies of their football heroes' shirts. In 1973 the Leicester-based company struck a deal with Don Revie, manager of Leeds United, who went on to win the 1973/74 league championship in a period when his team were dominant in England. The story is well told in Andy Wells's *Get Shirty.* Leeds United's commercial department was seen as making the maximum capital out of the club's success on the field, and Revie himself already had the unflattering nickname of 'Don Readies'[19] when Admiral came to call. The resulting deal guaranteed Leeds £10,000 a year in sponsorship, with Admiral receiving the profits from the shirt sales. It proved an immediate commercial success with other clubs, such as Norwich City, keen to bring in additional revenue, whilst displaying the manufacturer's logo as well as the club badge on the front of their shirts. From very early on there was criticism, however, over the cost of a complete set of a child's shirt, shorts and socks, which retailed at between £9.25 and £12.50 – about a third of an average weekly wage at the time.[20] Admiral, having made a critical breakthrough in ensuring that their nautical logo was clearly visible across the strips, didn't stop there. They also introduced their trademark on to the club's

17 Christopher Stride, Nick Catley and Joe Headland, 'Shirt tales: how adults adopted the replica football kit', *Sport in History*, 40.1 (2020). Available at: https://www.tandfonline.com/doi/pdf/10.1080/17460263.2019.1578255 (accessed 14 May 2025); Andy Wells, *Get Shirty: The Rise & Fall of Admiral Sportswear* (Conker, 2022); Alex Ireland, *Pretty Poly: The History of the Football Shirt* (Pitch Publishing, 2023).

18 Kevin Goodings, *Canary Threads: The Story of 50 Norwich City Shirts* (self-published, 2024).

19 Wells, *Get Shirty*, p. 49.

20 Ibid., p. 73.

tracksuits and even the holdalls that club physios used when they ran on to the pitch to treat injured players.

Admiral didn't stay the market leader for long, with other companies such as Umbro and Adidas keen to receive their share of the newly identified commercial opportunities. Academics identify the 1980s as when shirts started to appear in sizes suitable for adults. In Mac Mackay's column in the Norwich City programme for the match against Watford in March 1983,[21] the club's commercial manager noted that there had been requests from supporters for 'large size men's' NCFC shirts, and the first consignment was now available. 'Our Canary girl, Donna' was portrayed wearing the Canaries replica kit, though the shirts on offer were for boys, youths and men (no women's sizes), at prices from £14.99 to £20.99.

The scale of violence surrounding football during most of the 1980s no doubt delayed any growth in sales. It simply wasn't safe for fans to display their colours openly. The real breakthrough in sales came from 1989 onwards, when adults who were not players started to be used to model kits. Replica kits in women's sizes came much later. Sports clothing was assimilated quickly into fashion styles that could be worn away from the pitch and on the street. The advent of the Premier League, and football culture becoming 'cool', helped the football shirt become both a fashion statement and a label of allegiance to your club. By the 1990s replica shirts were coming to be the norm and were purchased by an older and more diverse group of fans. During this period it is reported that Umbro paid Manchester United £60 million for a six-year contract to manufacture their shirts.[22] Revenue opportunities were soaring.

Today's replica kit industry is huge, whilst production costs are low. Alex Ireland suggests that it costs less than £10 to produce, market and distribute a replica jersey.[23] Europe's leading clubs, such as Manchester United, are estimated to be selling around three million replica shirts a year.[24] Despite these hefty figures, Daniel Geey suggests that kit manufacturers nowadays usually take 80–90% of all revenue from shirt sales.[25] The clubs get their income from the upfront payments from the manufacturers. Thus, if a shirt retails for £60, the club is likely to be making £15 from each sale. Clubs now issue annual home, away and third strips, ensuring additional revenue streams.

21 'Mac's Scene', *Canary*, official matchday programme, Norwich City vs Watford, 2 March 1983.

22 Stride, Catley and Headland, 'Shirt tales', p. 27.

23 Ireland, *Pretty Poly*.

24 Wells, *Get Shirty*.

25 Geey, *Done Deal*.

Of course, fans have helped to create this market. Carrow Road and other stadiums are full of fans displaying 'their' colours. Whilst younger fans might wear a replica of what the players are wearing on the pitch, older supporters might choose 'vintage' jerseys, for which there is now a growing market, feeding on the nostalgia of those who grew up with the old Admiral strips of the 1970s.

Revenue from shirt sales is useful, but the value of sponsorship deals, whereby companies pay to have their brand displayed on the front of the shirts, is even more. Particularly if your club is in the Premier League, and your brand is being promoted, via television screens, to audiences across the world.

You Can Bet on Football to Take the Money

As the value of sponsorship has increased, a wider range of companies have seized the opportunity to promote their brands and products to football's huge following. Academics Remco Beek and Inge Derom describe sponsorship eras in the Premier League as reflecting changing industries and globalisation.[26] If anyone thought at the beginning that sponsorship was about philanthropy, they will swiftly have been disabused of those innocent early notions. The brands carried on the front of players' shirts are designed to promote commercial interactions. Or, to put it in less academic terms, they are there to sell fans something. Some of these products are pretty harmless. Football was used to sell Bovril from the end of the nineteenth century, and there is a strong tradition of the sport being associated with male grooming products, from Brylcreem to Nivea. Much less good for health, alcohol brands were ubiquitous in the early days of shirt sponsorship, from the iconic Liverpool FC shirts displaying Carlsberg's logo, to Norwich City's own partnership with Foster's lager (Norwich Brewery Company). But the explosion of gambling industry brands on to clubs' shirts and on to our television screens since the UK Gambling Act of 2005 has raised ever more serious questions regarding what is appropriate and acceptable.[27] Yet the football industry shows absolutely no sign of questioning where it takes its money from.

26 Remco M. Beek and Inge Derom, 'Sponsorship eras in the English Premier League: changing industries and globalization between 1992 and 2021', *Soccer & Society*, 23.4–5 (2022), pp. 349-366.

27 Chris Bunn, Robin Ireland, Jonathan Minton et al., 'Shirt sponsorship by gambling companies in the English and Scottish Premier Leagues: global reach and public health concerns', *Soccer & Society*, 20.6 (2019), pp. 824-835.

Sky Bet (part of Flutter Entertainment since 2020) has sponsored the English Football League continuously since the 2013/14 season. The deal was criticised from the beginning, with campaigners concerned about the impact this sponsorship might have on young people in particular. In 2017, when the deal was extended, Professor Jim Orford, an expert on gambling, was quoted as saying that the exposure of gambling brands to young people reinforced the 'normalisation of gambling'.[28] It should be noted that Norwich City announced that the Barclay Stand would be known as 'the Barclay Stand sponsored by Coral' (the betting company) in August 2015. The sponsorship deal was in place until the end of the 2017/18 season.[29]

Norwich City's exciting route to the Premier League after their play-off success in May 2015 was not followed by success back in the top tier. Their fluctuating fortunes were also reflected by changes in the board – Ed Balls became chairman in December 2015 (the former chairman, Alan Bowkett, had resigned). Robbie Brady was a significant pre-season signing (£7 million from Hull City). And in January 2016, in an effort to bolster the club's challenge, Lewis Grabban was recruited from AFC Bournemouth for a fee of about £8 million, followed by Ben Godfrey from York and Timm Klose arriving from Wolfsburg for £7.6 million. Steven Naismith was signed from Everton for a fee of about £8 million; Naismith is sometimes reported as Norwich City's biggest ever signing. Patrick Bamford also came on loan from Chelsea. Looking to the future, James Maddison was signed from Coventry City for a reported £2.5 million and was immediately loaned back to the Midlands club for the remainder of the season. At the end of the 2015/16 season, nevertheless, the club finished in 19th place and were relegated along with Newcastle United and Aston Villa. David McNally, no doubt frustrated at his inability to keep City in the Premier League, resigned on 9 May 2016 (a compensation fee of £1.35 million was subsequently paid to him by the club).[30]

Nathan Redmond was the first player to depart for what was reported as a club record fee of £11 million to Southampton, with Sergei Canós arriving from Liverpool for £2.5 million. Alex Pritchard and Nélson Oliveira joined in August. Results were not much better in the Championship though, after a promising start. Robbie Brady left for Burnley for another City record transfer fee of an estimated £13 million in January 2017. Alex Neil

28 Paul MacInnes, 'EFL's extended deal with bookmaker draws criticism from campaigners', *The Guardian*, 18 November 2017. Available at: https://www.theguardian.com/football/2017/nov/18/efl-football-league-sky-bet-new-deal-draws-criticism?CMP=Share_iOSApp_Other (accessed 28 May 2025).

29 Woodrow, *Norwich City Football Club*, vol. IV, 3 August 2015.

30 Ibid., vol. IV, 23 November 2016.

was dismissed in March (soon after a damaging 5–1 defeat at Sheffield Wednesday), to be replaced temporarily by first-team coach Alan Irvine. Norwich City appointed their first sporting director, Stuart Webber, in April 2017. City finished the season in eighth place in the Sky Bet Championship table (Newcastle United, Brighton and Hove Albion, and Huddersfield Town were promoted – the latter through the play-offs).

Norwich City away shirt, 2017/18 season (Sky Bet Championship. Norwich City home shirt, 2019/20 season (Premier League)

Author's collection

Webber was instrumental in the appointment of the first coach for the Canaries who was not from the British Isles. Arriving from Borussia Dortmund on 25 May 2017, Daniel Farke's job was to rebuild the squad and take Norwich City back to the Premier League.

Following nine years of sponsorship from Aviva, Norwich City announced a Swedish-based mobile gaming and sports betting company, LeoVegas, as their 'principal partner' in June 2017. The deal meant that the LeoVegas logo appeared on the front of team shirts, 'matchday training wear' and branding at Carrow Road. Norwich City's first home programme of the 2017/18 season (for the match against Sunderland) not unnaturally focused on the excitement around Farke's appointment. There were advertisements for both LeoVegas and Sky Bet, with an inside cover ad encouraging fans to download LeoVegas's 'super fast' mobile app. That last phrase illustrates many people's concerns about betting today. British gambling giant Bet365's innovative use of 'in-play' betting has enabled anyone with a phone to effectively have a 'betting shop in their pocket'.[31] Given that many fans watch a game these days on multiple screens in a pub, the constant inducements to bet can cause numerous problems, from financial issues to mental health crises.[32] Sunderland, Norwich's opponents in August 2017, were sponsored by Dafabet, another major gambling operator, this one headquartered in the Philippines.

Whilst Farke's Norwich only finished 14th in the Sky Bet Championship in 2017/18 (Wolverhampton Wanderers were champions), they fared significantly better in 2018/19. Farke's astute team-building was largely financed by the sale of James Maddison to Leicester City in June 2018 for a record estimated fee of £21 million. Norwich's pre-season signings that summer included Teemu Pukki, Emi Buendía, Moritz Leitner, Jordan Rhodes and goalkeeper Tim Krul. They joined academy team products

31 Robin Ireland, 'Champions League 2024: Uefa's decision to team up with a gambling giant will come at a high social cost', *The Conversation*, 17 September 2024. Available at: https://theconversation.com/champions-league-2024-uefas-decision-to-team-up-with-a-gambling-giant-will-come-at-a-high-social-cost-238273 (accessed 28 May 2025).

32 May van Schalkwyk et al., 'A public health approach to gambling regulation: countering powerful influences', *The Lancet Public Health*, 6.8 (2021), e614-e619.

LeoVegas
erreà
dafabet

Max Aarons and Jamal Lewis as key members of Farke's squad. City finished five points clear of Sheffield United in winning the Sky Bet Championship in May 2019.

Once again, the Canaries were back in the Premier League. Whilst LeoVegas had a three-year sponsorship deal with the club, City were able to break the contract if promotion was achieved. Shirt sponsorship which offers a Premier League audience is worth considerably more than the sums on offer to Championship clubs, and the deal with LeoVegas was therefore terminated. Norwich City were duly able to launch a 'record-breaking' shirt sponsorship deal with gambling operator Dafabet in July 2019.

Of course, from Norwich City's perspective the deal made absolute sense. The club's operating officer was quoted as saying that with 'Dafabet's history and longevity in sport sponsorship, we have an excellent partner to join us on our journey'.[33] With much of the Premier League's audience living across the world, gambling brand messages are often targeted at lucrative markets in Asia, sometimes in countries where gambling is banned. Dafabet was established in 2004 and has worked hard to build a profile in sport, but like many other gambling operators, it seems to have, shall we say, a complex and troubling mode of operation.[34] In 2021 Joey D'Urso published a devastating exposé of the practice of gambling firms using shirt sponsorship in the Premier League to 'facilitate illegal gambling'.[35] Perhaps it's time for football to put the health and well-being of fans before the additional income they can draw in from allowing gambling companies to showcase their brands at every single opportunity.

Whilst Premier League clubs have agreed a ban on shirt sponsorship by gambling brands from the 2026/27 season, this will only have a limited effect on the amount of exposure they have on our screens. The ban will not impact on the constant barrage of gambling advertising appearing on pitch perimeters or in football's accompanying social media content, for example.

33 Norwich City Football Club statement, 'City announce record breaking front of shirt partnership with Dafabet', 2019. Available at: https://www.canaries.co.uk/content/city-announce-record-breaking-front-of-shirt-partnership-with-dafabet (accessed 14 May 2025).

34 'Hyderabad cybercrime cops unearth global betting syndicate', *The New Indian Express*, 7 January 2024. Available at: https://www.newindianexpress.com/cities/hyderabad/2024/Jan/07/hyderabad-cybercrime-cops-unearth-global-betting-syndicate-2648696.html (accessed 14 May 2025).

35 Joey D'Urso, 'Special report: how Premier League shirt sponsors "facilitate illegal gambling"', *The Athletic*, 3 February 2021. Available at: https://www.nytimes.com/athletic/2361984/2021/02/03/gambling-premier-league-shirt-sponsors-investigation/ (accessed 28 May 2025).

Taking Fans for a Ticketing Ride

In 2011 respected journalist David Conn wrote that 'The Premier League has priced out fans, young and old.'[36] As he argued, since the break with the Football League in 1992, the money received from broadcasting and commercial income (including sponsorship and shirt sales) had transformed the game whilst increasing the price of watching it. Back in 1989 you could watch clubs such as Manchester United and Arsenal from the terraces for a ticket price of between £3.50 and £5 (£5 in 1989 is equivalent to £13.19 in 2025). A seat in the South Stand to watch Norwich City play QPR in Barclays League Division One in 1991 still cost only £3 (about £6.88 in today's money). Yet in 2011, Rogan Taylor was complaining that the cheapest adult price at all-seater Anfield was £45.[37] A ticket to see Norwich City take on Manchester United in the Lower Barclay Stand at Carrow Road cost £43. Of course, the grounds were safer and offered better facilities, but the increased cost of attending has priced out many younger supporters, and the average age of season ticket holders has got older.

Whilst matchday revenue is less important to the biggest clubs, as this is dwarfed by other income, it remains significant to smaller clubs such as Norwich City. Ticket prices today are often banded according to the opponents being played and cause considerable resentment amongst fans,[38] as they see corporate income being prioritised over them and their tickets. In 2017 10,000 Liverpool fans walked out when a £77 ticket was announced.[39] Protests about prices across different clubs continue today.[40]

The Americanisation of Our Sport

As already described, the selling off of English football clubs to foreign investors can be traced back to Roman Abramovich buying Chelsea in 2003. The American influence has become more prominent since the controversial

36 David Conn, 'The Premier League has priced out fans, young and old', *The Guardian*, 16 August 2011. Available at: https://www.nytimes.com/athletic/2361984/2021/02/03/gambling-premier-league-shirt-sponsors-investigation/ (accessed 28 May 2025).

37 Ibid.

38 Tommy Kweku Quansah, Babatunde Buraimo and Markus Lang, 'Determining the price of football: an analysis of matchday prices in the English Premier League', *European Sport Management Quarterly*, 24.3 (2023), pp. 764-784.

39 Press Association, 'Liverpool fans' walkout protest: around 10,000 leave in 77th minute over ticket prices', *The Guardian*, 6 February 2016. Available at: https://www.theguardian.com/football/2016/feb/06/liverpool-fans-walkout-thousands-ticket-price-protest?CMP=Share_iOSApp_Other (accessed 28 May 2025).

40 Football Supporters' Association, 'Supporters stand in solidarity over concessions and ticket prices', 26 September 2024. Available at: https://thefsa.org.uk/news/supporters-stand-in-solidarity-over-concessions-and-ticket-prices/ (accessed 14 May 2025).

purchase of Manchester United by the Glazer family in 2005. At the time of writing, Premier League Clubs Arsenal, Aston Villa, Bournemouth, Burnley, Chelsea, Crystal Palace, Fulham, Leeds, Liverpool and Manchester United and Fulham are all under majority American ownership. Perhaps more surprisingly, *The Athletic* reported in 2023 that 22 English Football League clubs have American investment, from Millwall to Wycombe, Portsmouth to Barnsley.[41] And of course there is Wrexham, bought by American actor Rob McElhenney and Hollywood star Ryan Reynolds, in a process that itself sounds like a fantasy story.[42] In contrast, the German Bundesliga only has one club under foreign control (RB Leipzig).

The increasing involvement of American owners reflects how open our football clubs are open to overseas investment. And the Americans are in it to make money, although of course this involvement does not always bring results. Crawley Town's experience with WAGMI United has not been entirely successful, although perhaps things are turning round.[43] American owners also bring their own ideas on how the sport should be run. The proposal for a breakaway European Super League in April 2021 had initial strong support from Joel Glazer (Manchester United), John W. Henry (Liverpool) and Stan Kroenke (Arsenal). Guaranteed fixtures against the likes of Real Madrid and Juventus are always going to sound more attractive than run-of-the-mill Premier League matches against Sheffield United, Norwich City or Burnley.

And we have seen already how television dictates kick-off times. Super Sunday and Monday Night Football, both introduced with the advent of the Premier League in 1992, are American TV imports. However, Martin Calladine, rather interestingly, notes that not all things about American sport are bad.[44] For example, American football (the NFL) maintains competition between teams by ensuring that TV money is shared equally, imposing a strict salary cap on its players, and using a draft system to ensure that the worst teams get first pick of the best new players. However, there is always going to be a perceived clash between American marketing and management strategies and English traditions of the game.[45] A North American focus is likely to encompass the widest possible maximisation of diverse revenue streams.

41 Nancy Froston, '22 EFL clubs have been invested in by Americans – this is how they are getting on', *The Athletic*, 26 December 2023. Available at: https://www.nytimes.com/ athletic/5148257/2023/12/26/efl-clubs-american-ownership/ (accessed 14 May 2025).

42 Ian Herbert, *Tinseltown: Hollywood and the Beautiful Game: A Match Made in Wrexham* (Headline, 2023).

43 Froston, '22 EFL clubs have been invested in by Americans'.

44 Martin Calladine, *The Ugly Game* (Pitch Publishing, 2015).

45 John Nauright and John Ramfjord, 'Who owns England's game? American professional sporting influences and foreign ownership in the Premier League', *Soccer & Society*, 11.4 (2010), pp. 428-441.

Norwich City will find out soon enough the extent to which they might benefit (or not) from American involvement. In September 2022 Mark Attanasio and his Norfolk FB Holdings group became a minority stakeholder and director at the club. In October 2024 Delia Smith and Michael Wynn-Jones's twenty-eight-year period as majority shareholders came to an end, and Attanasio's American group assumed overall control of Norwich City.

Global Digital Connections

A global society presents more challenges and opportunities for football clubs seeking both to grow their market and to stay connected with their fans. By the end of the 1990s, Premier League clubs already had established websites, but the development of social media has changed digital engagement dramatically. In 2010 Norwich City welcomed new director Stephen Fry[46] (Fry resigned as a director in January 2016 to become 'Norwich City Ambassador') [47] and focused on his embrace of Twitter as a means of communication.

Today, Facebook, X (formerly Twitter), Instagram, YouTube and TikTok all provide platforms for marketing. Much of the interaction between fans and clubs enables relationships to be mutually beneficial. Whilst in the 1970s, fans used transistor radios to keep up with match scores, today's information sources are instant and multifaceted. Fan engagement is positive and enables up-to-date information on players and match information, but a significant amount of club activity is devoted to revenue-generating actions.

At the same time, sponsors can work with clubs to drive purchase of their products. Various academic studies have illustrated how pervasive gambling companies' methods are, for example. FUN88, a gambling company founded in China and targeting audiences in Asia, Europe and South America, used their shirt sponsorship of Newcastle United to promote gambling and general business globally,[48] and they used Twitter extensively to draw on Newcastle United's rich history whilst encouraging the club's fans to bet on match results.

Clubs such as Manchester United and Liverpool have huge digital followings extending their fanbase across the world and into lucrative

46 See *OTBC*, Norwich City matchday programme, Norwich City vs Swansea City, 21 August 2010.

47 Woodrow, *Norwich City Football Club*, vol. IV, 18 January 2016.

48 Robin Ireland, 'Brand engagement in a digital age: marketing gambling to Newcastle United fans', in Darragh McGee and Christopher Bunn (eds), *Gambling and Sports in a Global Age* (Emerald Publishing, 2024).

markets in Asia and North America. By focusing on video content, YouTube and TikTok have enabled clubs to gain large numbers of new followers, primarily amongst younger audiences.[49] In the period between July 2023 and July 2024, Liverpool stacked up an incredible 221 million views on their YouTube channel. Meantime, Manchester United had 38.2 million followers on their English X account in October 2024. There are undoubtedly many other accounts in different languages. Their commercial department's aim will be to monetise that following whenever they can. In 2019 *Forbes Magazine* wrote that Manchester United claimed to have 253 million fans and followers in China, and had partnered with China's Alibaba to send the club's content across Alibaba's platforms.[50] The partnership included United having a store on Tmall, Alibaba's online marketplace, so that they could sell club merchandise direct to Chinese fans. Meanwhile, Norwich City had 876,900 followers on X in October 2024.

At a Time of Crisis, Questions are Asked.

On 17 August 2019 Norwich played their first match of the season at Carrow Road, against Newcastle United, still managed then by Steve Bruce (the game ended in a 3–1 victory for City with a hat-trick for Teemu Pukki). The match programme reads like many others at the start of a new season. Daniel Farke and Norwich's City's executive committee focused on the fans and the importance of the relationship between 'the Yellow Army and the team'. The big story on the pitch was the first use of VAR at Carrow Road. There was also a piece about the new LED ribbon on both the Regency Security Stand and the Barclay End which replaced the old scoreboards. Whilst the programme noted that these would help communication at the ground, the more cynical amongst us appreciated that this would also enable more opportunities for the sponsors to display their brands. And these were self-evident in the programme, including Dafabet's full-page spread on the inside cover, a page on insurance brokers and financial planners the Alan Boswell Group, an advertisement for Woodforde's Brewery, a 'primary partner', and a subscription offer from Green Farm Coffee. Aviva had a nice piece

49 Football Benchmark, 'Social media insights from the 2023/24 club football season', 11 July 2024. Available at: https://www.socialfootballsummit.com/en/shl-social-media-insights-from-the-2023-24-club-football-season/ (accessed 28 May 2025).

50 Sam Pilger, 'Manchester United continue to build on their dominance in China', *Forbes*, 11 December 2019. Available at: https://www.forbes.com/sites/sampilger/2019/12/11/manchester-united-continue-to-build-on-their-dominance-in-china/ (accessed 28 May 2025).

on tackling loneliness in Norwich. And of course, Delia's Catering was promoting its tasty offers at Carrow Road. Dafabet's logo on the team's shirts ensured that the gambling company was featured in different ways throughout the programme.

Farke's astute management, supported by Stuart Webber and backed by a board still chaired by Ed Balls and including Delia Smith and Michael Wynn-Jones, had brought Norwich City back to the Premier League in August 2019. However, the season ahead was to call into question all aspects of the modern game. The bare facts about the coronavirus pandemic are easy to document. The first case documented in the UK was on 31 January 2020. From then through to autumn 2021 there were waves of infections, marked by the emergence of new variants of the virus, including alpha, gamma and omicron. There were national lockdowns from March to June 2020 and January to July 2021. There were also local lockdowns in place between September and November 2020. Gatherings and movement were restricted to all but essential venues and hospitality venues were closed. Football clubs, like all other parts of UK society, were put under the microscope and their activities closely examined.

The rising number of coronavirus cases started to affect the staging of matches in March. The fixture between Manchester City and Arsenal due to take place on 11 March was postponed due to concerns over contacts made by Arsenal players with Olympiakos's owner, who had tested positive for the virus. Arsenal had played the Greek club in the Europa League earlier that month. Remarkably, the match between Liverpool and Atletico Madrid was allowed to take place on that same date, despite the growing number of cases in Madrid. Supporter Simon Hughes covered the match for *The Athletic* and wrote about his experience in November 2021.[51] The piece clearly showed both how the fixture contributed to the spreading of the virus on Merseyside, and the human cost attributed to this. The game turned out to be the last football match on English soil for over three months.

The English Premier League suspended its 2019/20 season on 13 March 2020 – the first time a season had been suspended since the advent of the Second World War. Premier League fixtures did not resume until 17 June, with matches then taking place without fans being permitted

51 Simon Hughes, 'Liverpool vs Atletico Madrid. The match that changed everything', *The Athletic*, 2 November 2021. Available at: https://www.nytimes.com/athletic/2917494/2021/11/02/liverpool-atletico-madrid-champions-league-match-that-changed-everything/ (accessed 28 May 2025).

to attend. The restrictions remained in place throughout most of the 2020/21 season except on a very few occasions in December 2020 and in May 2021. It was a time when clubs' business interests were juxtaposed closely against the welfare roles that they have traditionally played within their communities.

Norwich City did their best to navigate the crisis, as did all other football clubs. Early on they took a decision to furlough their staff in an effort to mitigate costs.[52] But as the crisis developed, the club focused more on supporting the Norwich and Norfolk community. Following the Premier League's Restart Programme which focused on assurances to keep the players safe, the season resumed on the weekend of 19–21 June with all matches played behind closed doors, and all the remaining matches in the season to be televised.

Match Report: Friday 19 June 2020, k/o 18:00. Premier League, Carrow Road, Norwich City 0 Southampton 3. Match originally scheduled for 14 March. Attendance: Television audience only.

Norwich City
Tim Krul, Max Aarons, Ben Godfrey, Timm Klose, Jamal Lewis, Emi Buendia (Adam Idah), Kenny McLean, Tom Trybull (Mario Vrancic), Todd Cantwell (Onel Hernandez), Teemu Pukki (Ondrej Duda), Josip Drmic (Josh Martin). Head Coach: Daniel Farke.

Southampton
Alex McCarthy, Ryan Bertrand, Jan Bednarek, Jack Stephens, Yan Valery (Kyle Walker-Peters), Nathan Redmond (Sofiane Boufal), Pierre-Emil Højbjerg, James Ward-Prowse, Stuart Armstrong (William Smallbone), Michael Obafemi (Che Adams), Danny Ings (Nathan Tella). Manager: Ralph Hasenhűttl.

Goals
Southampton: Ings (49), Armstrong (54), Redmond (79)

Two programmes were produced for the match between Norwich City and Southampton in the 2019/20 season. The first was for the original fixture date on 14 March. In this programme the impending coronavirus

52 'Pay cuts, furlough or deferrals: what are the Premier League clubs doing?', *The Guardian*, 2 April 2020. Available at: https://www.theguardian.com/football/2020/apr/02/pay-cuts-furlough-or-deferrals-what-are-the-premier-league-clubs-doing (accessed 14 May 2025).

pandemic does not get a single mention. Football continues, with the outside world firmly kept outside. Just ten days earlier, on 4 March, 9,000 Norwich City supporters had been at Tottenham's magnificent new stadium for their FA Cup fifth round fixture. Thanks to Tim Krul's heroics, they witnessed an epic penalty shootout victory and a quarter-final place. In the excitement around this, it is worth reflecting that it had been twenty-eight years since the Canaries had last travelled this far in the FA Cup (when Sunderland beat Norwich in an FA Cup semi-final at Hillsborough). In the 1970s and 80s the Canaries were able to regularly enjoy cup runs, before the financial realities of today's Premier League kicked in, with the later rounds of the cup competitions now only usually enjoyed by the select moneyed few.

Back in the Premier League, things were already challenging for Daniel Farke's team. City were bottom of the table, four points behind Aston Villa, who had played one game less, and six points behind Watford who were occupying 17th place, the final position above the three clubs in the relegation zone. The Canaries were facing Southampton, who had shown that recovery was a possibility. The south coast team had remarkably lost 0–9 at home to Leicester City in late October and were then in the bottom three with eight points from ten games. But a run of good results (assisted by the goal-scoring of Danny Ings) meant that Southampton were now in 14th place, and 13 points above Norwich. However, the Canaries still had nine games left to play. A positive result against Southampton could change everything. The day before the match was due to take place, the Premier League postponed its season due to the pandemic; it took the UK government until 23 March to impose a full lockdown. It could be said that the League reacted earlier in order to protect its fans, players and staff.

We no doubt all remember where we were and how we faced this unprecedented period in our lives. Many of us lost family and close friends to the pandemic. Some of us lost jobs and our children suffered in isolation from their playmates and from school. Efforts to restart the economy and indeed normal life were placed under the microscope almost immediately. The Premier League's Project Restart was challenging, and some players were understandably nervous about the risk to their or their family's health. The matches that took place over 19–21 June were staged behind closed doors, with Farke and club captain Grant Hanley using the match programme to describe the efforts to ensure that people's health and safety were put first at all times. Even producing a programme for a match without fans in the ground required an explanation. Dan Brigham, the programme editor, wrote, 'We felt it was the right thing to do to produce a matchday programme for those who want to get as close to a matchday experience as possible without actually being at Carrow Road.'

The image used on the front cover was of two simple clasped hands reflecting the hashtag slogan printed at the top of the programme, **#APARTBUTTOGETHER**. *At the top right there was a heart containing an NHS logo with the statement, 'Norwich City thanks all NHS, care, and essential workers for your amazing efforts.' Inside, the two-page spread on the work of the club's Community Sports Foundation amplified how a football club is able to promote health and well-being at a time of crisis. The COVID-19 Community Project benefited from over £200k donated by players, senior staff and directors. Some of its work is described below, as taken from the match programme:*

- *Over 7,000 calls made to older and vulnerable season ticket holders by club and Foundation staff, including 300 calls made by first-team players*
- *2,500 care packages delivered so far containing around 75,000 items*
- *Packages and support for over 20 local charities*

In an unprecedented situation, all the remaining matches of the Premier League were to be shown on free-to-air channels (for example, Sky used their Pick channel). The matches were shown with artificial crowd noise although you could watch without that if you so chose. The clubs themselves could use five substitutes per match instead of three. This rule change has remained, favouring the richer clubs with deeper squads.

It was an unreal situation but, like other fans, I tuned into my television with some hope of a positive result from a game Norwich needed to win to have any chance of staying up. The sober and difficult time was reinforced by the television coverage showing the players 'taking the knee' and with 'Black Lives Matter' printed on the back of their shirts as a gesture of solidarity following the murder of George Floyd.

In the end, the football was a dreadful anti-climax. As the headlines said, 'Southampton hammered bottom side Norwich City'. Watching the match live felt like watching a coaching session or a turn-out for the reserves. It was 0–0 at half-time, with the only action of note being a clipped shot by Danny Ings on to the top of the crossbar. Ings made amends early in the second half with a strong curling shot into

Front cover of match programme, Norwich City vs Southampton, 14 March 2020. Subsequently postponed due to COVID-19

A second programme for the same fixture which was eventually played behind closed doors on Friday 19 June 2020

Author's collection

#APARTBUTTOGETHER

the top right-hand corner of the net. Just five minutes later, Armstrong made it 2–0 with a low left-foot shot from just outside the area. The mood was flat and it felt like game over. Not just in this match but for Norwich's latest efforts to stay in the Premier League. Twenty-five minutes later Nathan Redmond scored Saints' third against his former club to complete the Canaries' capitulation.

Norwich City lost all nine of their matches during Project Restart and were relegated on 11 July with three games still remaining after losing 0–4 at home to West Ham United. When they played at Arsenal on 1 July, the Arsenal programme cover poignantly displayed the images of some of their fans who had lost their lives during the pandemic.

The Action Had to Continue – The Cameras Had to Roll

BBC Radio Norfolk's Chris Goreham reflected on what a match would be like without fans in the Southampton programme. And in July, the BBC reported on how clubs had tried to build an atmosphere to accompany the TV screenings of matches in empty grounds.[53] The efforts made by TV companies and by clubs included masking empty seats with cardboard cutouts of fans and piping in artificial crowd noise. Of course, it was no substitute for the real thing.

In efforts to ensure their sponsors were happy, clubs went to great lengths to display banners where spectators would normally be sitting. For example, Newcastle United ensured that their shirt sponsor FUN88 received as much exposure as possible; gambling companies came under the spotlight, with one match including 716 separate exposures to gambling logos.[54] In Norwich's game against Southampton, it was impossible to miss the multiple exposures to Dafabet's logo and other gambling brands such as Betway. When a few fans were allowed back in at Tottenham Hotspur, they were seated in an upper tier stand, reportedly so that television cameras were able to capture banners in lower-tier areas showing advertising for a gambling company, energy

53 'Zoom walls, fake crowd noise, water breaks: did you enjoy lockdown football?', BBC news, 27 July 2020. Available at: https://www.bbc.co.uk/sport/football/53504214 (accessed 14 May 2025).

54 See Channel 4, 'Football's Gambling Addiction', aired 7 June 2021; Rob Davies, 'Gambling logos feature 700 times in football match, says C4 documentary', *The Guardian*, 5 June 2021. Available at: https://www.theguardian.com/society/2021/jun/05/gambling-logos-feature-700-times-in-football-match-says-ch4-documentary#:~:text=Football's%20Gambling%20Addiction%20airs%20on,and%20then%20available%20on%20All4 (accessed 14 May 2025).

drinks and unhealthy snacks.[55] And it seemed to work: the Gambling Commission's consumer research data showed an increase in gambling activity during lockdown.[56]

Spectators were not allowed back into stadiums for almost the entire 2020/21 season. Nige Tassell captured the Championship season in his entertaining book, *The Hard Yards*.[57] Norwich City were one of the clubs that were able to admit a small number of fans into the ground in September 2020 – 882 supporters were able to watch a 2–2 draw at Carrow Road against Preston North End on 19 September – and again in December – a maximum of 2,000 home supporters were permitted to watch games against Sheffield Wednesday, Nottingham Forest and Cardiff City – all wins. But it didn't last; most clubs were unable to allow fans into grounds until the 2021/22 season. Daniel Farke led Norwich to their second Sky Bet championship in three years, six points in front of Watford. Brentford were promoted through the play-offs. Tassell quoted the club's ex-striker, Chris Sutton, on his assessment of both the season and the club's future chances: 'They want to be successful, but the truth of the matter is that they're never going to be able to compete with the Manchester City's and the Chelsea's and the Liverpool's over the course of a season.'[58] Already crowned champions, Norwich City wore a special edition kit for their final home match against Reading in May 2021. It featured a montage of fan images, but no sponsors' logos; it was intended to symbolise how much the club were missing their fans at Carrow Road.

It Isn't Always About the Money

The decade had reinforced the 'haves' and the 'have-nots' of the Premier League. And Norwich City, like almost every other club outside football's historical heartland of north-west England, and the financial colossus of the capital city, were never able to compete at the top level for much longer than a season.

55 Ben Nagle, 'Tottenham fans fume at Daniel Levy and owners ENIC for putting returning fans in the upper tier in order to keep sponsorship banners next to pitch ... while charging them £60 for the privilege – the most expensive of any team in the Premier League', *Mail Online*, 20 May 2021. Available at: https://www.dailymail.co.uk/sport/football/article-9599565/Tottenham-fans-SLAM-Daniel-Levy-owners-ENIC-decision-returning-fans-upper-tier.html (accessed 14 May 2025).

56 Gambling Commission, 'Data showing the impact of Covid-19 on gambling behaviour', 4 May 2021. Available at: https://www.gamblingcommission.gov.uk/news/article/data-shows-the-impact-of-covid-19-on-gambling-behaviour-using-operator-data#:~:text=The%20number%20of%20bets%20(12,lasting%20more%20than%20one%20hour. (accessed 28 May 2025).

57 Nige Tassell, *The Hard Yards: Triumph, Despair and Championship Football* (Simon & Schuster, 2021).

58 Ibid., p. 200.

NORWICH CITY FC

As American and other foreign investment has poured into the Premier League and, indeed, into some other Football League clubs, English football has become a global entertainment product. Games are played in England but with the majority of players originating from outside the United Kingdom, and with kick-off times sometimes designed to suit spectators on the opposite side of the world. It seems that television and sponsors' demands have become more important than those of fans.

And yet the coronavirus pandemic showed that football had not entirely lost its soul. Clubs remembered the parts they had historically played in their local communities. When fans were not permitted into grounds, television and club executives moved swiftly to try and find a way to create an atmosphere whilst they kept their sponsors happy.

'Norwich A Fine City'. The special edition shirt dedicated to their fans, worn by the Norwich City players for their final home match of the 2020/21 season against Reading on 1 May 2021

Author's collection

177

'And that's the thing now: you've got to be commercial.'

Delia Smith, February 2025[1]

Afterword

The pandemic seasons of 2019/20 and 2020/21 gave the football world pause for thought: many were able to reflect on the national game and the relationship between clubs and fans. But if they were hoping that there might be changes in how football would look in the future, they were to be severely disappointed as life gradually began again.

Even before the UK government had enforced the lockdown on 23 March 2020, Jűrgen Klopp, then manager of Liverpool FC, said that we all have a duty to protect each other and help people stay healthy. As he wrote, 'football always seems the most important of the least important things'.[2] And of course, Klopp is right about football, but that resolve to protect each other certainly wobbled across the pandemic seasons, as it did across all sections of society. The chase for money often trumped public health. Liverpool FC's owners, along with the club's fierce rivals, Manchester United, were keen to seize any business opportunities the pandemic might present. On 12 October 2020 Project Big Picture tried to provide the biggest clubs with even more control over the Premier League, reducing the size of the competition, and allowing more time to play in expanded European competitions, whilst sweetening the deal with a payment to the English Football League to cover lost revenues in 2019/20 and 2020/21.[3] The proposal was vigorously rejected after criticism from the government and the Football Association. Project Big Picture was followed in April 2021 by England's biggest clubs, along with 12 more from Europe, planning to launch a European Super League. Once again, this power grab was rejected after football fans made their feelings very clear.

Player card, (Panini)

Author's collection

1 Delia Smith quoted in Martin Samuel, 'The full story of Delia Smith's 28 years in charge of Norwich City', *The Sunday Times*, 22 February 2025.

2 Jűrgen Klopp, 'Jűrgen Klopp's message to supporters', *Liverpool FC*, 13 March 2020. Available at: https://www.liverpoolfc.com/news/first-team/390397-jurgen-klopp-message-to-supporters (accessed 14 May 2025).

3 Matt Slater, 'Explained: Project Big Picture – The winners and losers', *The Athletic*, 12 October 2020. Available at: https://www.nytimes.com/athletic/2132829/2020/10/13/project-big-picture-premier-league-efl/ (accessed 20 May 2025).

Community Values

For Norwich City fans, there was a sharp reminder that the 'community values' that the club had demonstrated to their fans in 2020 now seemed misplaced. The club was preparing for a new season back in the Premier League: life in the top flight had made the club more valuable to potential sponsors, and in June 2021 Norwich City duly announced a shirt sponsorship deal with Asian online betting company BK8. Within hours fans were noting that BK8's marketing on social media in South-Eastern Asia involved the use of scantily clad young women. It caused a furore – 'This is Norwich City, not Sin City'[4] – and the club was forced to back down. On this occasion, the club's values and its relationship with its fans were prioritised above revenue. A new deal was swiftly struck with Lotus Cars, whose headquarters are in Bethel, Norfolk: a sponsor who had backed the club before and whose image fitted better with Norwich City.

The season kicked off in earnest in August 2021, when the Canaries welcomed the previous year's Premier League runners-up, Liverpool, to Carrow Road. The pandemic had not been entirely forgotten, with positive tests for COVID-19 affecting some of the pre-season preparation. The match programme noted that it was the 50th anniversary of the 1971/72 season when Norwich City first reached the 'Holy Grail' of the First Division. Overall, the mood was very positive for the Liverpool game. If nothing else, the welcome back to fans to a sold-out stadium was heartfelt. But by five o'clock on that Saturday afternoon, reality had set in, after another easy 0–3 win for the Merseyside club. By November, just three months later, Daniel Farke had been dismissed, but life was no easier for his successor, Dean Smith. Norwich City finished the season in 20th and last position and were duly relegated.

Same As It Ever Was

So this book was completed in June 2025: Norwich are preparing for their fourth successive season in the Championship, now wearing their Norfolk clothing company (Blakely) sponsored shirts, under freshly appointed Norwich-born head coach, Liam Manning, and their longest spell in the second tier of English football since 2009; Dean Smith

4 Chris Lakey, 'This is Norwich City, not Sin City', *Pink Un*, 10 June 2021. Available at: https://www.pinkun.com/news/22694450.norwich-city-not-sin-city/ (accessed 14 May 2025).

was followed by David Wagner, and then Johannes Hoff Thorup, none achieving significant success; meantime the Canaries' former manager, Daniel Farke, is preparing for his third attempt to survive in the Premier League with his new club, Leeds United. Norwich will be joined in the Championship by upwardly mobile, US celebrity-backed Wrexham and Birmingham City. And English football remains firmly set on its money-laden path: a global entertainment product sold to the highest bidder, whether that is Hollywood, American asset-strippers such as the Glazers, or the sovereign wealth fund of Saudi Arabia.

Mind the Gap

Watford, who were promoted in 2021 along with Norwich, also faced a swift return to the Championship. This is now the reality for many of the promoted clubs from the Championship, who have very little chance of competing, let alone staying, in the Premier League. The three clubs that were promoted from the Championship in 2022/23 – Burnley, Sheffield United and Luton – were all relegated in 2023/24. Exactly the same happened the following season to the three promoted sides – Leicester City, Southampton and Ipswich Town – despite the fact that both Southampton and Ipswich had each spent around £100 million in the summer of 2024 trying to guarantee survival. The huge revenues enjoyed by the big clubs such as Liverpool and Manchester City make it practically impossible for the likes of Norwich City, Watford, Ipswich and Southampton to have any long-term future in the Premier League, unless it's grubbing around in the bottom few places seeking to grab points wherever they can. There was an exception in 2022/23 when Nottingham Forest spent more than £150 million on over twenty new players. And whilst they were docked four points for breaching the Premier League's Profit and Sustainability rules, the strategy clearly worked on this occasion.

There is an argument that Norwich should compare themselves with clubs like Brighton, Brentford, and Bournemouth, but these have now been in the top tier for several seasons enabling them to benefit from years of inflated revenues derived from broadcasting contracts and becoming the "Premier League middle-class".[5] Cup victories in 2025 for Newcastle United (the EFL Cup) and Tottenham Hotspur (Europa League) are

5 Michael Walker, 'Will Sunderland and the newly promoted teams fare better than this season's instant returns', *The Athletic*, 26 May 2025. Available at: https://www.nytimes.com/athletic/6381132/2025/05/26/sunderland-premier-league-leeds-burnley-promoted/ (accessed 9 June 2025).

scarcely victories for the underdog (however unexpected) given those clubs' annual revenue figures, but Crystal Palace winning their first major trophy (the FA Cup) in 115 years is perhaps a more encouraging story with their fairytale triumph over Manchester City at Wembley.

When Liverpool were declared Premier League champions in 2025, it brought an end to Manchester City's run of success. Yet Liverpool are one of only seven clubs to win the Premier League since its formation in 1992, and it is unlikely that the title will be won in 2026 by any club other than Liverpool, Manchester City or Arsenal. That being said, between 1972 and the start of the Premier League, there were also only seven winners of Division One, with Liverpool dominating proceedings in the 1970s and 80s with 11 titles. Derby County under Brian Clough were, however, title winners in both 1972 and 1975. As County's club legend from that era Roy McFarland has said, in those days it was possible for clubs like Leeds United, Burnley and Ipswich Town to challenge the big-city clubs of London, Liverpool and Manchester.[6] But the financial gap between, say, Manchester City, Norwich City and Derby County has become huge. In 2023/24, Manchester City's revenue was £715 million, Norwich's was £73.1 million and Derby's (then in Division One) was £19.4 million. No regulator is going to smooth out those chasms. Even finishing bottom of the Premier League can be a financial win. Sheffield United's single season in that same football year of 2024 provided a nice little earner of £109.7 million.

Follow the Money

The Labour Party's landslide election victory in July 2024 might not have been greeted by the same fanfare that welcomed Tony Blair's victory in 1997; and, just as twenty-seven years previously, the new government has not signalled any significant change in economic direction. Hopes for any closing of the gap between the haves and have-nots in society have not been fulfilled thus far.

Similarly, there are fears that the new Independent Football Regulator, introduced as part of the Football Governance Bill, will not be able to fully address the huge financial inequalities between the Premier League and Football League clubs. However, the government's preferred candidate did at least say publicly in May 2025 that the financial preservation of

6 Michael Walker, 'Derby County, the Premier League title race and the death of variety', *The Athletic*, 23 April 2025. Available at: https://www.nytimes.com/athletic/6263548/2025/04/23/premier-league-title-winners-derby-liverpool-leeds/ (accessed 20 May 2025).

the football pyramid was critical.[7] A planned root-and-branch review of English football directly followed the anger that resulted from the failed proposal for a European Super League in 2021. The regulator has an important role in trying to improve financial sustainability and in vetting potential new owners of clubs and investors. It also opens the door for this and future governments to ensure that the Premier League does not only consider its own interests but is obliged to take a wider look at football across the board.

However, the game has changed and clubs will inevitably continue to prioritise corporate income and monetise every aspect of the game that they can. After all, if they don't, they will be at a financial disadvantage with respect to their competitors. Whilst Keir Starmer can access free tickets at Arsenal, the Football Supporters Association is renewing its call for fairer ticket pricing in the Premier League, using the hashtag #StopExploitingLoyalty. In October 2024 it reported that Premier League prices had gone up by around 7%, with concessionary prices for younger and older supporters being particularly affected. In 2025 Liverpool fans claimed that ticket prices had risen 800% since 1990.[8] Manchester City did not endear themselves to many of their fans when they announced a deal with the online ticket site Viagogo in March 2025. It sounded like yet another way to market resale match tickets to well-heeled overseas tourists. It even costs more to watch matches on television as the number of broadcasters and streaming services continues to rise.

The Premier League is still huffing and puffing about any possible government interventions in 'its' competition, although it is clear that the previous government smoothed the way for the Saudia Arabia-backed takeover of Newcastle United in 2021. At the same time, the legal battle between Manchester City and the Premier League over 'associated party transaction' (APT) rules has serious implications for future financial fair play.[9] In February 2023 the Manchester club was charged with 115 counts of breaching the Premier League's financial rules. Basically, APT rules, which were introduced by the Premier League in December 2021, seek to

7 Paul MacInnes, 'Clock ticking on Premier League and EFL redistribution deal, warns new regulator', *The Guardian*, 7 May 2025. Available at: https://www.theguardian.com/football/2025/may/07/clock-ticking-on-premier-league-and-efl-redistribution-deal-warns-new-regulator (accessed 20 May 2025).

8 Andy Hunter, 'Prices have risen 800% since 1990': the Premier League fans' unions campaigning for affordable tickets', *The Guardian*, 6 January 2025. Available at: https://www.theguardian.com/football/2025/jan/06/prices-have-risen-800-since-1992-the-premier-league-fans-unions-campaigning-for-affordable-tickets?CMP=share_btn_url (accessed 20 May 2025).

9 Matt Slater, 'Manchester City vs the Premier League: who do lawyers think won the APT case?', *The Athletic*, 15 October 2024. Available at: https://www.nytimes.com/athletic/5839725/2024/10/15/manchester-city-vs-the-premier-league-who-do-lawyers-think-won-the-apt-case/ (accessed 20 May 2025).

prevent clubs from benefiting unfairly from, for example, a sponsorship deal with a company associated with its board. Since their Abu Dhabi United takeover in 2008, Manchester City - who play their matches at the Etihad Stadium - have benefited from sponsorship and partnerships with Abu Dhabi-based (and often state-owned) airlines, banks, telecoms companies, hotels, real estate and energy companies.. The legal argument surrounds whether the commercial income from these arrangements was valued more highly than it should have been and thus created an unfair advantage for the club. At the time of writing, this court case has still not been fully resolved. You can imagine that these kinds of legal arguments will surround the richest clubs in Britain for years to come, much like the battles around where Amazon pays its taxes and how social media giants such as X (formerly Twitter) can be regulated. The richest in society will always fight tooth and claw using the best legal advice money can buy to argue that their riches have been legitimately gained.

In the same way that the very wealthy seem to avoid paying tax through any means at their disposal, football clubs will use every loophole possible to avoid getting caught up with the Premier League's Profit and Sustainability rules. Having been relegated in 2020, AFC Bournemouth were promoted as runners-up in the EFL Championship in 2022 and have not only retained their place in the Premier League, but have been moderately successful, reaching the FA Cup quarter-finals in 2025 before being beaten by Manchester City. This success story has its home at Dean Court (or the Vitality Stadium as it is now known for sponsorship purposes), which has a capacity of 11,307. Clearly it is not ticket sales or fan power which is keeping the Cherries in the top league. They were able to throw money into staying up as the club's £71.4 million debt was written off after they were bought by yet another American consortium, the Black Knight Football Club group, in December 2022.[10] Sports journalists now have less need for literature degrees than a good grounding in economics.

For those Premier League clubs who are able to access FIFA's latest golden bauble – the Club World Cup (launched in June 2025) – this is surely a World Super League in everything but name. Chelsea, who finished 4th in the 2024/25 Premier League table, will be rewarded with £40 million if they manage to get out of the group stage. As in the world in general, we are creating a football super rich who live in their own rarefied and protected sporting world.

10 Dan Sheldon and Chris Weatherspoon, 'Explained: how Bournemouth avoided a PSR breach and what it means for other clubs', *The Athletic*, 10 April 2025. Available at: https://www.nytimes.com/athletic/6269182/2025/04/10/bournemouth-psr-premier-league-rules/ (accessed 20 May 2025).

LOTUS
Growth, Integrity, Belonging, Resilience, Pride, Commitment

Remember the Fans

'There's two ways to look at it. One is that the Premier League is the best in the world and everybody lauds us and our competition, but in another way we've lost so much of what football is. I think that's a bit sad.'
Delia Smith, February 2025[11]

As with most of Britain's traditional industries, our football clubs are now often owned by overseas interests. Norwich City are the latest to fall into that category. For many fans, this is a positive. After all, Delia Smith and Michael Wynn-Jones are not billionaires. And you need to be a billionaire to help your club compete in this new cut-throat football world. There will be other fans who look back with some sadness and fondness on the values and culture that Norwich City's former owners seemed to represent. But there are warnings for us all to see. For the Premier League to remain successful as a source of global entertainment, it needs its fans, and it needs to be competitive. That is still the hope for Norwich City and for many other clubs across England.

There are some fans though who see the Premier League as fundamentally uncompetitive. The title and the relegation places were sewn up a long time before the end of the 2024/25 season. Sitting at Preston railway station in January 2023, after Norwich had demolished North End 4–0, I bumped into a Burnley supporter whose team were riding high in the Championship and indeed finished champions by no less than 10 points (ahead of Sheffield United). I congratulated him on his team's success. His retort was that he was not looking forward to a return to playing in the Premier League. He expected Burnley to lose heavily and their players to be outmuscled and outplayed; there's not a lot of fun in that after all. And here we are again in 2025, with Burnley, who were indeed relegated after one season in the Premier League in 2023/24, about to have another go in the land of riches and giants.

I am not nostalgic for the racism and violence which accompanied English football in the 1970s and 80s. And I wouldn't pretend that the sport wasn't commercial even in those days. But it was very hard to make serious money until 1981, when directors could draw salaries from clubs and dividends were no longer capped. The game has changed irrevocably as broadcast revenues have soared and gambling sponsorship has poured in, whilst billionaires and foreign states have bought up clubs that used to be accurate representations of their fans and communities. Match

11 Delia Smith quoted in Samuel, 'The full story'.

times reflect television needs and ticket prices have rocketed, and they are harder to obtain. Profit comes before anything else, including fans.

Norwich City as a Bellwether Club

In March 2025 journalist Daniel Storey described Norwich City as 'the bellwether club in English football',[12] and I find it quite hard to disagree with him. The old model of English owners that Delia Smith and Michael Wynn-Jones represented has long gone. Indeed, some Norwich supporters have argued that Smith and Wynn-Jones outstayed their welcome and should have given way earlier to allow new money in. So, here we are in 2025 with more new American owners seeking to make a buck from English football's heritage and tradition.

In 2018 Norwich saw relegation as part of a long-term strategy, using parachute payments to gain promotion again and gradually consolidate in the Premier League. But by finishing Championship winners and Premier League wooden spooners in sequence across four seasons, they were perhaps the first club to illustrate the widening gap between the top two divisions. Their strategy now, like that of so many other clubs, is data-driven, drawing on the identification of young talented players who they can develop and then sell on.

It seems ironic to quote Norwich City's much-maligned former chairman, Robert Chase, who, in a letter written to shareholders in March 1996, argued, 'We cannot normally expect our trading activities to produce a profit unless at the same time we are able to maintain a successful transfer policy which involves moving on players to allow new and perhaps more promising players to develop.'[13] Perhaps not so much has changed after all: the sums and the risks remain the same. Yet the ridiculous and frankly unhealthy amounts of money now in the game have distorted the market so much that the chances of the Burnleys, Derby Countys, Norwich Citys and Ipswich Towns of this world succeeding in the Premier League are now very slim indeed. A sign of the times is that some supporters of these clubs (including myself) have started to dread promotion from the Championship – if and when it happens. There is so little chance of competing and there is no pleasure in getting hammered at regular intervals by the 'big boys'. In truth, English football is now

12 Daniel Storey, 'Norwich City sum up 21st century English football better than any other club', *The i Paper*, 7 March 2025. Available at: https://inews.co.uk/sport/football/norwich-city-21st-century-english-football-3569291?ito=link_share_article-top (accessed 20 May 2025).

13 James Woodrow (as compiled for the Norwich City Football Club), *Norwich City Football Club: The Archive* (Severn, 2022), vol. III, 11 March 1996.

a lesser game, and surely for many it is less enjoyable to watch. The financial excesses of today's Premier League have created a real-life tragedy. Greed has triumphed, and football's historic communities and their fans have been sidelined.

And yet, in putting this book together, it's the memorable matches across the decades that really mean something – not the money Norwich may or may not have accrued from them. For a club like Norwich – and there are many – the joy is so often in the journey rather than the destination. The possibility of a great team coming together out of seemingly nothing and in so doing bringing a community together too.

The hope that this will happen again, that Norwich will have another unexpectedly memorable season, is what keeps me and many others coming back. Hope, in this increasingly commercialised and monetised game, might seem like an impossibly naive concept. But, seeing families weep with sheer communal joy as Crystal Palace won the FA Cup in 2025 for the first time was a reminder of what football can do for a community – and what we stand to lose if we ignore what it really means in the pursuit of money.

Acknowledgements

I realised the need for a book like *Cutting the Mustard* while undertaking the initial research for my PhD on the English Premier League at the University of Glasgow in 2017. Why, when people constantly complained about the commercialisation of football and the widening financial gaps dramatically affecting the sport's competitiveness, was it so hard to document the key factors in how the elite professional game in England had changed since I started watching Norwich City in 1972?

So, first of all, I need to acknowledge the support I received from colleagues at the university to undertake my academic research. Thank you, Chris Bunn, Stephanie Chambers, and Gerda Reith.

When I realised that this book couldn't just be a list of dates and facts, and needed to involve a much larger footballing community, a group of friends and colleagues (including everyone at the Health Equalities Group) assisted in my thinking and helped with my writing. Mark Allerton, Andrew Bennett, Bob Bennett, David Blane, Beth Bradshaw, Nicola Calder, Mike Carey, Richard Glendenning, Gary Gowers, Charlotte Morris, Matthew Philpott, Annie Rosewarne, Ed Stacey, Michael Viggars and Michael Wood, all indulged me in various conversations online and in-person. And those good researchers and historians at the International Football History Conference, the Football Collective and the National and Scottish Football Museums made me feel it was worthwhile.

In researching Norwich City, the Centenary Edition of *Canary Citizens* was essential as was the marvellous and frankly remarkable, *Norwich City Football Club Archive.* Thanks so much to the wonderful NCFC Historical Trust, and James Woodrow in particular, for enabling me to access this historical treasure trove, once I'd connected with Andrew Johns who kindly passed on his copy to me.

Over the years I have attended Norwich City games with a wide variety of people, some of whom are no longer with us I'm afraid. Particular thanks for joining me on my Norwich City supporting journey must go to David Arthur, Rob Butcher, Ian Gibson, Phil May, Geraint Parry, Tim Roderick, Jim van Wyk, Seb Ward, James Wells, and Don and Tom Williamson, and all members of the fabulous Northern Canaries supporters' group (and other NCFC fans across the UK whom I have met in my various footballing journeys).

Andrew Kirk did some exemplary copy-editing. Any remaining mistakes however should be firmly ascribed to me alone!

This book would not have existed at all without the thoughtful design skills of Alan Ward at Axis Projects, and the wise writing and communications talent of Ben East, both fellow Canaries. Thanks also to my elder daughter, Boglarka Szabo, for her great work in setting up www.robinireland.com. Both Boglarka and her sister, Flora, can always be relied on for giving me sound technological and social media guidance.

And of course, when you write a book your nearest and dearest suffer most. My heartfelt thanks to Rebecca, Bogi and Flora for putting up with me. And none of you even like football!

The last word goes to Rebecca who I would like to thank for the endless proof reading and all her help and support; she even came up with the book's great title!

Thank you to everyone. I hope you enjoy the book. OTBC.

About the author

Photo: AJW

Robin Ireland is an academic, writer and football fan. All these things came together in the creation of *Cutting the Mustard*, showing how money has changed football for ever. Ireland's academic career took him from his first degree at the University of East Anglia back in 1977, through his Master of Public Health at the University of Liverpool and his PhD and current position as Honorary Research Fellow in the School of Health and Wellbeing at the University of Glasgow.

The season ticket which was my prize for winning Norwich's first Fantasy Football League in 1998/99

Author's collection

From first arriving in Norwich in 1972 to study for his A-levels at Norwich City College, Ireland has followed Norwich City Football Club, even winning the first Fantasy Football League the club organised in 1998/99 as an indication of what some may describe as an obsession. Ireland has cheered the Canaries at Carrow Road and the San Siro, from the Pirelli Stadium to Easter Road.

His writing has always accompanied him on his academic and football journeys. Ireland has been published previously in the *British Medical Journal* and the *Bulletin of the World Health Organisation*, as well as in *Soccer and Society* and *Sport in Society.*

Cutting the Mustard is Ireland's second book, and follows *Sport, Sponsorship and Public Health*, published by Routledge in 2023.

For more information: www.robinireland.com